Kill or Cure?

Kill or Cure?

How Canadians can remake their health care system

Dr. Carolyn Bennett
and Rick Archbold

A Phyllis Bruce Book
HarperCollins*PublishersLtd*

Kill or Cure?

How Canadians can remake their health care system
Copyright © 2000 by Carolyn Bennett
and Rick Archbold.
All rights reserved. No part of this book may
be used or reproduced in any manner what-
soever without prior written permission
except in the case of brief quotations embod-
ied in reviews. For information address
HarperCollins Publishers Ltd,
55 Avenue Road, Suite 2900,
Toronto, Ontario,
Canada M5R 3L2

www.harpercanada.com

HarperCollins books may be purchased for
educational, business, or sales promotional
use. For information please write: Special
Markets Department, HarperCollins Canada,
55 Avenue Road, Suite 2900,
Toronto, Ontario,
Canada M5R 3L2

First HarperCollins hardcover ed.
ISBN 0-00-200057-1
First HarperCollins trade paper ed.
ISBN 0-00-639101-X

Canadian Cataloguing in Publication Data

Bennett, Carolyn (Carolyn A.)
Kill or cure? : how Canadians can remake
their health care system

"A Phyllis Bruce book".
Includes index.
ISBN 0-00-200057-1

1. Health care reform — Canada.
2. Medical care — Canada.
I. Archbold, Rick, 1950– .
II. Title.

RA449.B44 2000   362.1'0971   C00-931257-9

00 01 02 03 04 HC 5 4 3 2 1

Printed and bound in the United States
Set in Monotype Joanna

For my patients and family
whose caring has shaped mine.

Contents

Preface

In 1994, when I first decided to run for public office, my patients complained, "We're going to lose a good doctor." But I had no trouble explaining my decision: "I think I have to go and do this in order to make sure that it continues to be possible to be a good doctor!" I told them. By then our health care system seemed ready to crumble, putting stress on both patients and health care providers. Instead of looking for ways to make our system sustainable—by spending money more efficiently and paying more attention to preventing sickness in the first place—governments chose primarily to put a lid on costs. They began rationing medical services to save money, and succeeded mainly in eroding Canadians' confidence in their system.

Canadians are justifiably proud of their universal, publicly funded medical care system. It is a distinctive part of our country, one of the ways we show to ourselves and the world that our values include caring for one another and a fundamental sense of fairness. Reforming medicare involves much more than economic choices and policy choices. It involves making a choice about our values as a nation. I've made my choice. The kind of health care system I want for me and for my children is one that makes no distinctions between rich and poor, a system under which all Canadians are equal.

Kill or Cure?

These days, an increasing number of politicians and others are arguing that the only way to save medicare is to sell off large chunks of it to the private sector. Many people, inside and outside the medical profession, will never be happy until patients have to pay. They believe against all the evidence that patients need deterrents in the form of user fees in order to stop them from "abusing" their system.

These proponents of what is often called a "two-tier" system argue that a parallel system of private providers will "take the load off the public system." What's more, they say, these private operators will inject a healthy dose of competition into the health care marketplace that will help control costs and lead to better service. I don't buy these arguments, as I explain in the pages that follow. But, equally important, these arguments camouflage a very different set of values from the ones on which our universal public system was founded, values that have to do with equity, social justice, and the public good.

When I first ran for public office in Ontario, I promised my patients I'd work to remake a health care system they believed in, one that reflected their values. I believed then and I believe now that the confidence that Canadians have in the public health care system is our ultimate protection against those who want to push us down the slippery slope to a two-tier, American-style system. I am convinced that Canada's approach to health care is fundamentally sound. But the message that the system needs fixing, not trashing, isn't getting through. I left my wonderful practice to make sure that the message was delivered loud and clear to the people making the decisions.

Six years later, I'm in Ottawa, and still working to bring the view from the trenches into the corridors of power. But I also now realize that the future of health care won't be secured by one—or even seven!—physicians sitting in the House of Commons. Our system will be reformed in a sustainable way only if we reset the table where decisions are made and allow patients a permanent seat at that table. Their priorities and the way the system affects them must come first.

Last year I ran into author and *Globe and Mail* national columnist Jeffrey Simpson at the annual "Politics and the Pen" dinner in Ottawa. Jeff had heard me ranting about health care reform and now he issued a challenge: "What makes you think that Canada can be the only industrialized nation with a universal health care system?" "Because Canadians want it to work," I replied. As I explained to him that day, I believe that Canadians want us to fix the system and keep it publicly funded and equitable. Our system of universal health care is a Canadian badge of honour. Canadians don't want to let it go; they want to help make it work.

Canadian health care is at a crossroads. We are in the midst of a national debate that will determine the kind of system we take into the twenty-first century. Will we fix the system that has served us well for many years, but that isn't working so well any more? Or will we let it slip away? Will we take collective action to cure what ails Canadian health care or will we kill it through ignorance and inaction?

I have written this book to help frame the health care debate that heated up during the winter of 1999–2000 and that will undoubtedly simmer on for years to come. I believe the debate should not be about *whether* we can afford a publicly funded system—evidence from around the world overwhelmingly shows that public systems are better and more efficient than private systems or two-tier systems—the debate should be over *how* to reform the Canadian medical system so that it delivers top-quality care to all of the people all of the time. So that it provides every Canadian citizen with the level of health care he or she needs and deserves.

Michael Ignatieff once remarked that one of the real barriers to any progressive movement is a nostalgic look back to some *perceived* paradise in the past. Medicare past was no paradise: many of its problems were disguised because we simply threw money at them. That approach won't work any more. Given the tools—above all, the information— Canadians in their roles as knowledgeable patients, effective advocates, and committed citizens can and will make our system work. They have to. I promised my patients, the people of St. Paul's, and Jeffrey Simpson.

Part One

The System

1

Is It Safe to Get Sick?

Is there really a crisis?

Canada's health care system has long been considered one of the best in the world, delivering a high quality of care to any person who needed it, at little or no cost beyond the payment of annual income taxes. It was universal, accessible, and publicly funded. No matter where in the country Canadians travelled, they had immediate access to care and were treated just as well as if they'd never left home. We Canadians had such faith in our system that it became part of the way we defined our country, of how we defined ourselves as a people. As former Health minister Monique Bégin has observed, our system "grew out of our particular history and political culture." Maurice Strong, former executive coordinator of the reform effort for U.N. secretary-general Kofi Annan, has noted that the cold countries around the top of the globe were the first to establish a government-sponsored social safety net, including universal health care. Perhaps because we live in a cold country with vast spaces, we naturally developed a more communal value system than that devised by our neighbours to the south. For whatever reason, we believe in looking after one another and helping the least advantaged. Our health care system epitomizes what is best about our country.

You'd never guess this from the recent news reports of the

crisis in emergency rooms or the worrying waiting list problem or the fight in Alberta over the provincial government's plan to allow private clinics to perform various operations formerly available only in public hospitals or the stories about the flight of some of our best doctors and best-trained nurses to the United States. A visitor to Canada in the winter of 1999–2000 would have concluded from reading the daily newspapers that the Canadian health care system was on the verge of a nervous breakdown. It wasn't, and it isn't. The serious problems getting all the media attention don't change one essential truth: Canada's system is still one of the best in the world. Just look at how we stack up.

The best way to rate the quality of Canadian health care is to compare our "health outcomes" with those in other countries in the developed world—the twenty-nine countries, including the United States, that belong to the Organization for Economic Cooperation and Development (OECD). With the exception of the United States, all OECD countries have some form of publicly funded universal health care system. The statistics the OECD collects from its members include various measures of health outcomes—numbers that tell us how healthy a population is, and when and how people get sick.

To me, two of the most revealing sets of statistics are those that track perinatal mortality and life expectancy. In both categories Canada ranks near the top of the list. Let's look first at perinatal mortality, the rate at which babies die at birth or in the first week after birth. Perinatal mortality has declined dramatically during the twentieth century, since the arrival of antibiotics. Yet from country to country these mortality numbers vary widely. In 1996, the last year for which complete OECD figures are available, Canada's perinatal death rate was six per thousand. In the United

States, the rate was almost eight per thousand. One fascinating side effect of the recent Elian Gonzales custody battle in the United States was the revelation that Cuba, despite being a developing nation, has a perinatal mortality rate half of that in Washington, D.C. Since baby death in the first week after birth is a good indicator of the care the mother received during pregnancy, the difference in infant mortality suggests that Canadian mothers got better health care than their U.S. counterparts.

The figures on life expectancy are even more startling. According to the United Nations' *Human Development Report* 2000, Canada ranked third in the world, after Japan and Iceland, in life expectancy at birth. The United States ranked twenty-fifth. Our newborns can be expected to live until the age of 79; theirs, till only 76.7.

The life-expectancy data become even more interesting when you look at how they vary with income. In Canada, life expectancy varies with income, but not nearly as much as it does in the United States. In the United States, poor people live much shorter lives than the better-off. The largely private system in the United States means that those who can afford to pay get much better care than those who can't. Canada's relative health equity doesn't excuse the shocking disparity in life expectancy between our aboriginal people and other citizens. But it does suggest that we are in a better position to do something about it.

Taken together, the statistics on perinatal mortality and life expectancy make Canada look good in comparison with the United States. But what about the rest of the developed world, especially countries that have systems closer to ours? The United Nations' *Human Development Report* 2000 yet again ranked Canada the best country in the world in which to live. It contains a section called "Health Profile," which tabulates statistics measuring a number of health outcomes, from the rate of measles immunization of one-year-olds to the number of doctors and nurses for every 100,000 people. Among those countries with "high human development," including Norway, Japan, Sweden, the United Kingdom—and the United States—Canada ranked first. For example, Canada, Australia and Iceland have virtually eliminated maternal mortality, while in the United States eight women die per 100,000 live births—the same as Portugal.

On the face of it, then, the Canadian health care system seems to be doing a reasonable job of keeping us healthy— a measurably better job than the system to our south. What's more, it does so at a substantially lower cost. For as long as the OECD has been keeping statistics, the United States has spent far more on health care per capita than any other member country, which means it spends far more than any country in the world. In 1997, the Americans spent $4,095 per person on health care. We spent just over half that amount, $2,175. In short, we get better health care for less money than the Americans. And we have a universal system. They don't.

These comparisons don't change the fact that our system is having problems, just like the health care systems in almost every other country in the developed world. Like Canada, most OECD countries have for the past decade been struggling to control costs. These cost pressures stem from the advent of expensive new drugs and expensive new technologies, and from the gradual increase in life expectancy. People are living longer; the longer they live, the more they use their health systems over the course of a lifetime. Some of the problems also stem from the way health care is changing as we move from a more hospital-centred system to a more community-based model.

Whether a country's system is a pure example of socialized medicine, like Cuba's national health system, or a predominantly private system, like the one in the United States, or a mixture of the two, health care is changing and the change is often painful. Among the developed world's systems, Canada's sits somewhere in the middle, with a mix of public and private elements. For example, while most of our doctors are reimbursed by the government for their services, most are self-employed, not public-sector employees.

Canada's system is unique in being the only one where all core health insurance is publicly funded. Regardless of whether the provider is a privately owned walk-in clinic or a publicly owned hospital, the government pays for your care. Canada's approach is often described as a single-payer, comprehensive health insurance system. Other countries—even Great Britain—have a mix of public and private systems both in insurance and in delivery. Such systems are often called two-tier systems.

Among the health care systems in greatest peril these days is Great Britain's. During the Thatcher years, government cutbacks so eviscerated the National Health Service that it recently veered close to total breakdown. Health care spending in Britain helps explain why. Where Canada now spends more than 9 per cent of its gross national product (GNP) on health care and the United States spends more than 14 per cent, the British spend less than 8 per cent. To save the British system, Prime Minister Tony Blair recently announced that his government would put £20 million in new money into the National Health Service over the next four years. But he took pains to point out that the new money would be spent on making the system better, including a serious commitment to long-term health goals such as reducing the incidence of heart disease, not on applying Band-Aids.

Australia, whose system in some ways resembles ours, is also having its troubles. Australia's system has grown increasingly two-tiered in recent years, allowing private acute-care hospitals to operate alongside public ones. Doctors, who can move back and forth between the private and public systems, have quickly learned how to work the two tiers for their benefit. For example, Australian surgeons continue to use the public system when they have more expensive operations to perform. Then they walk across the street to the private hospital to perform simpler procedures at steep rates. The private hospitals also charge a premium over the public system for high-demand tests such as magnetic resonance imaging (MRI) and high-demand therapies such as radiation for cancer. The Toronto Star's Thomas Walkom reported after visiting Australia last winter that "patients willing to pay hefty extra fees to these hospitals and to Australia's well-heeled specialists can jump the queue."

Compared with the system crisis in Britain and the increasingly two-tier system in Australia, Canada's health care system is reasonably stable. But we Canadians have no reason to be complacent, as last winter's emergency room overload demonstrated. It's important, however, to put our recent problems in perspective. As Michael Decter, director of the Canadian Institute for Health Information (CIHI), has pointed out, the crisis in the winter of 1999–2000 had three major causes: "The first is the annual flu epidemic, which, this season, created more business for hospitals as Christmas holidays were taken by doctors and nurses. Peak demand met skeleton staffing. The second is the absence of flexibility in a hospital system squeezed for nearly a decade. The third is the lack of alternatives to the emergency room—in reality, the lack of sufficient investment in the Canadian health care system of the future."

More interesting to me than the cities that drew all those headlines are the ones that didn't. The Capital Region Health Authority (CRHA) in Edmonton, Alberta, had no emergency room pile-ups. How come? Because it put together a coordinated plan for the winter "high" season. The CRHA's chief clinical physician, Dr. Robert Bear, brought in all the stakeholders—nursing homes, community clinics, family physicians—and made them part of the planning process. During the late fall, nursing homes made sure all their staff and residents got flu shots. Before the winter crunch hit, a crisis team was in place. Each day during the critical flu season, the team monitored all the hospitals in the region and directed patients to those with available beds. Every one of the CRHA's member hospitals had a home-care coordinator stationed in its emergency room who could send many people right back where they belonged—at home—but make sure they got the care they needed. A similar approach met with similar success in Calgary and Saskatoon.

One of the few Toronto hospitals that experienced only minor emergency room problems in early 2000 was the Hospital for Sick Children. Sick Kids has done something very smart: it has a twenty-four-hour-a-day telephone triage system. Instead of packing your feverish child off to the emergency room down on University Avenue, you call a special number where a triage nurse, someone trained to decide how urgent a case is, listens to your symptoms and tells you whether you really need to come in right away or can wait until the doctor's office opens the following day.

Toronto's Hospital for Sick Children aside, emergency room problems tended to be worst in big cities, and worst of all in our biggest city, Toronto. Ontario, with its highly centralized but very poorly integrated health care system, is not a model to emulate. In the words of Duncan Sinclair, until recently the chair of the Ontario Health Services Restructuring Commission, "We have now, in effect, a single, humongous (and distressingly ineffective) 'integrated' health system in Ontario. Everyone who carries an Ontario health card is a member. It is too big and poorly organized for its size." As Decter, Sinclair, and many others have argued, it is not simply a question of money; it is a question of how the system is organized.

Perhaps the best single description of the current state of Canadian health care came from the Prime Minister's National Forum on Health in its 1997 report to the federal government. The forum focused on four areas for improvement: pharmacare, home care, information technology, and primary-care delivery. Its report concluded that "the fundamentals of Medicare are sound and that the Canadian health care system must continue to be founded on the bedrock of the single-payer publicly financed model." And that this system will be preserved only by "doing things differently and making decisions based on better evidence." As the Ontario Hospital Association argued in November 1998 when it appeared before the House of Commons Standing Committee on Finance Pre-Budget Consultation, "The underlying problem is thoughtless mechanical tinkering with the system in nearly every province . . . The crisis is rooted more in faulty planning than demographics, finance or technology. The good news is that this management problem can be fixed."

This "thoughtless tinkering" arose in response to the sorts of pressures I alluded to above—an aging population, expensive new therapies and medical technologies and, of course, the reduction of transfer payments—some of the many pressures that health care systems are experiencing as they attempt to re-create themselves for the twenty-first century. In Canada, the resounding theme of this tinkering has been holding the line on costs. As my friend Mary Eberts, former chair of the Ontario Task Force on Midwifery, has said to me more than once, "When the debate is only about costs, it misses the point entirely. If we now spend $25 billion on an inefficient system, we won't make it more efficient by spending $18 billion. Conversely, if we simply increase what we spend on health care without looking at efficiency, we may simply get more expensive and equally inefficient care. The real challenge is how to get the best care for each public dollar we spend."

According to the recently released *World Health Report* 2000 from the World Health Organization (WHO), that's exactly where our system is failing to make the grade: we aren't getting good enough value for the health care dollars we spend. Significantly, the authors of the report took the broadest possible definition of a health system, namely, "all the activities whose primary purpose is to promote, restore or maintain health." That not only includes all sickness care, home care, traditional health promotion, and disease prevention, but health-related education, including changes in the school curriculum that would make students better future caregivers and more responsible consumers of health care.

As the report stated, "Health systems consist of all the people and actions whose primary purpose is to improve health. They may be integrated and centrally directed, but often they are not. After centuries as small-scale, largely private or charitable, mostly ineffectual entities, they have grown explosively in this century as knowledge has been gained and applied. They have contributed enormously to better health, but their contribution could be better still, especially for the poor. Failure to achieve that potential is due more to systemic failings than to technical limitations. It is therefore urgent to assess current performance and to judge how health systems can reach their potential."

When Canada's whole system is looked at in this light, it doesn't look nearly so good. Overall, the *World Health Report* 2000 ranked us thirtieth in the world. But much of that surprisingly low ranking stemmed from the failure of our system to live up to its potential—given our resources and the amount of money we already spend. Canada came twelfth overall in level of health (measured in disability-adjusted life expectancy), eighteenth in health distribution (there are still too many disparities between regions and economic groups), seventeenth to nineteenth in fairness of financial contribution (30 per cent of our health care is purchased with private dollars), and seventh in overall attainment of health care goals. If the quality of Canadian health care is generally high, however, it isn't nearly high enough given how much we spend. Our health expenditure per capita in international dollars ranked tenth, but our health performance rating (based on what we could have achieved with the same resources) was thirty-fifth. That's how we ended up in thirtieth place overall. (France placed first; the United States placed thirty-seventh.)

On the day the report was released, a WHO analyst on CBC *Newsworld* concluded succinctly that Canada was not getting value for the money it spends. I rest my case! We must stop evaluating our health care system by how much we spend and start rating it according to results. As my dad used to tell me before he would agree to raise my allowance, "First you've got to explain how you spent what

I was already giving you." Simply spending more money on health care won't solve anything in the long term.

Before we can reform our health care system, we've got to understand clearly where and how it isn't working. And to do this, we need to remember where our system came from and how it has evolved.

A brief history of Canadian medicare

Most Canadians know that publicly funded health care started in Saskatchewan in the late 1940s, when Tommy Douglas formed the first CCF government in Canada. (The CCF later joined other political groupings on the left to become the New Democratic Party.) In 1946, the Douglas government passed the Hospitalization Act, which funded public insurance for hospital care. In 1957, the federal government of John Diefenbaker brought in the Hospital Insurance and Diagnostic Services Act. This federal statute committed Ottawa to cover half the cost of any provincial hospital insurance program, as long as that program was comprehensive, universal, and accessible, and its coverage was portable (i.e., public health insurance covered you outside your home province). Soon, other provinces began to follow Saskatchewan's lead. So far, however, public health insurance covered only hospital stays.

In 1962, Tommy Douglas did it again, making Saskatchewan the first jurisdiction in North America to include visits to the doctor's office under a tax-supported insurance scheme. (The legislation was passed, but not before 90 per cent of the province's physicians went on strike.) By 1971—near the end of Pierre Trudeau's first term as prime minister—the foundation of our current system was firmly in place. In essence, it was a system of universal health insurance. It assumed that 99 per cent of health care was delivered either by hospitals or by individual doctors working outside a hospital setting.

A number of items weren't covered unless you were on welfare, were over sixty-five or under the age of twelve: ambulances; drugs prescribed outside the hospital; dental care; optometry. And there were, and are, some variations among provinces. In most provinces Workers' Compensation still operates as a separate health care insurance plan. And some Canadians get their health care directly from the federal government: military personnel and war veterans; aboriginal people living on reserves; members of the RCMP. Still, Canadians could claim with some justification that they had a universal system. Nobody could have predicted that, between 1971 and 1990, our basic system—public insurance for care provided by hospitals and doctors—would begin to erode as the definition of health care expanded and as care increasingly moved into the community and became much more multidisciplinary.

Here's how Monique Bégin recently described what happened: "We started learning that health was much more than physicians and hospitals. Health promotion and disease prevention, healthy life-styles and active living, primary care, became part of the vocabulary. We also witnessed the appearance of institutional user fees or extra-billing by physicians. The notion of a two-tiered system, that of double standards, as well as the arguments against public health insurance (socialized medicine as waiting lists and low quality care; patients as abusers of the system; the brain drain of physicians), shook the political class and nurtured a public debate for at least five years, longer in Ontario. The public witnessed, and participated in, the first serious round of attacks against the system since its inception."

Bégin is referring here to the battle over extra-billing (doctors who were charging each patient a fee above that paid by the provincial insurance plan had become a particular problem in certain specialties such as anesthesia and orthopedics) in the early 1980s, which led her to introduce the Canada Health Act of 1984. The act banned extra-billing and brought in strict penalties for provinces that failed to prohibit the practice. After three years and some $245 million of cash penalties imposed on seven provinces (reimbursed after they corrected the situation), extra-billing disappeared, but not before a series of nasty strikes by doctors in Ontario and elsewhere. For the time being, Canadians were satisfied that extra charges were not to be tolerated. As Bégin puts it, "Canadians' attachment to their beloved No. 1 health care system had been reinforced in the process."

Unfortunately, the second half of the 1980s did not witness a commitment to redesigning our system for a changing society. Instead, both the federal and the provincial governments threw more money at the existing system, with no measurable benefits. Between 1980 and 1990, Canada's per capita expenditure on health care doubled without any noticeable improvement in the quality of care. (As I argue later in this book, in large part the reason was the complete lack of fiscal accountability in the system. For example, when hospitals ran deficits, the government simply paid the difference.)

When this explosion in costs ran into a wall in the form of the recession of the early 1990s—the longest and deepest economic downturn since the Great Depression of the 1930s—something had to give. Government budgets, including health care budgets, did the giving. During this era of deficit reduction, governments at every level could no longer simply throw more money at every health care problem.

The System

Both the federal government and the provinces committed less money to the social safety net, of which health care is a primary part. But instead of looking for ways to save money by making the system work better, the object became simply to cut costs.

The desire to cut costs ushered in the "de-listing" of services defined as not "medically necessary," a subtle but steady erosion of the universality of the publicly funded insurance system. Next came hospital "restructuring," as provinces closed beds and shut down or merged hospitals in an attempt to save money by "rationalizing" the hospital sector. Apart from the well-documented dislocations these closures caused, they also accelerated a trend already well under way: the shift of health care away from hospitals and into the community. This shift brought with it an unintended additional cost to health care consumers: many drugs that would previously have been prescribed by doctors in hospitals, and thus paid for by public health insurance, were now being prescribed outside hospitals and so had to be bought by the patient. In some cases co-payments or user fees were applied for patients on a government drug plan. In provinces where the move to health care in the community was neither well planned nor funded, community resources, including caregivers at home, were stretched well past their limits.

In the hospital sector, one of the most glaring side effects of restructuring was the shortage of medical technicians in some key areas. For example, a serious shortage of radiation therapists prompted Ontario and Quebec, among several provinces, to aggressively recruit abroad, while several provinces paid to send patients to get these treatments in the United States.

By the late 1990s, everywhere Canadians looked, their

health care system seemed to be worse off than a decade earlier. They read the sensational news stories about problems inside hospitals themselves and the lengthening waiting lists and the reports of shortages of nurses and doctors, and wondered whether all Canadian health care was in crisis. In fact, the very real problems were signs of haphazard and wrong-headed reform and of a system that hadn't caught up to twenty-first century realities. Despite all those scary headlines, it is still safe to get sick in Canada—at least for most of us, most of the time. Those newspaper headlines were signs of a system that needed to be radically reformed, not abandoned. As the WHO report dramatically illustrated, we need to remake our health care system to ensure value for our dollars. We need to do things differently.

2

Fixing a Failing System

Our patchwork system today

I sometimes describe the current state of health care in Canada as a patchwork quilt of non-systems. We don't so much have a health care system as we do a system of health insurance. This publicly funded insurance pays for services provided by both public institutions (hospitals) and private practitioners (doctors). Within the limits laid down by the Canada Health Act, each province can spend its health care dollars as it sees fit and organize its health care delivery any way it wants. In true Canadian fashion, every province is different, and within provinces there are all sorts of variations.

Some provinces insure some of the cost of prescription drugs for all their citizens. Others cover only drugs for seniors and those on welfare. Procedures that have been delisted in some provinces are still covered in others. Most provinces have set up regional health authorities, devolving a great deal of the administration of their system from the centre to the regions. Ontario still runs its system entirely from the centre. Quebec has placed great emphasis on community-based clinics. Alberta is trying to privatize part of its system (a topic I return to in chapter 10). As Michael Decter has astutely observed, "In Canada, we have a system for financing health care. But we've never had a system for delivering health care."

A patchwork of non-systems means a system of loosely connected sectors that often work at cross-purposes. Deliverers of acute care (hospitals), chronic care (home care programs and nursing homes) and primary care (family doctors and community clinics) often communicate poorly and seldom coordinate their efforts. When it comes to prescription drugs—which now account for more health care dollars than do physicians' services!—we are all over the map. Before the age of sixty-five, most Canadians have to pay for their own prescription drugs, unless they're prescribed in a hospital. As a result, I remember patients being admitted to hospital by sympathetic doctors so that they wouldn't have to pay for their medications, not because they needed to be there. And so it goes. Ours is a system of many solitudes.

Despite this often chaotic situation and the many differences among provinces, one can make certain generalizations about the way health care in Canada is currently being delivered to its clients. I'd say that the most important generalization reflects the continuing shift from hospital to non-hospital settings. As I've already mentioned, this shift was well under way before the massive wave of restructuring that led to the recent rash of hospital mergers and closings and was speeded up by the disappearance of hospitals and hospital beds. In the year 2000, much more medical care is delivered outside hospitals than a decade ago—by family physicians, public health nurses, in community clinics, or in a patient's own home. According to the Canadian Institute for Health Information (CIHI), in the last decade the hospital sector's use of total health care dollars has shrunk from over 42 per cent to just over 30 per cent.

In my opinion, the recent country-wide emergency room crisis happened as a direct result of the way in which hospital restructuring was done. We radically and abruptly downsized the hospital sector before we'd prepared the non-hospital sector to fill the vacuum. Michael Decter uses an apt metaphor to describe what happened: "Imagine if our banks had closed thousands of branches and then, several years later, began installing ATMs. The lineups at the remaining branches in the transition years would have been vast and intolerable." Yet that's exactly what we did with the hospital sector.

As the success of cities like Edmonton and Winnipeg at avoiding the emergency room crisis suggests, the root cause of the problem was less a matter of dollars than of inefficiencies in the system. Emergency rooms in January 2000 were clogged with people who didn't belong there, people who didn't need acute care. But, regardless of the reason, hospitals are becoming less important as we shift the delivery of a great deal of care into the community, which is where it belongs.

What about the other foundation stones of the original system: individual doctors and nurses? What does their world look like in the year 2000? Since nurses are too often overlooked, or taken for granted, when we talk about health care, let's consider them first. What we see is not a happy sight. Perhaps more than any other sector of Canadian health care, nursing is in crisis. Hospital restructuring cost thousands of nurses their jobs. Too many of those that remain have been turned into casual, part-time workers whose irregular hours and lack of attachment to a single institution or department means they can't possibly deliver the continuum of care they want to provide and for which they have been trained. It also means that teamwork suffers. Studies have shown that it takes six months for a health care team to gel. You can't build an effective team without a strong core of full-time staff that works predictable shifts.

No wonder nurses are leaving the profession in record numbers or moving to better-paying jobs in the United States. No wonder the profession is growing steadily older and not renewing itself. We have 15 per cent fewer nurses than a decade ago, yet the long-term need for nurses is growing, especially in the expanding world of community-based health care. According to André Picard, in his recent book on the state of Canadian nursing, *Critical Care*, "it is projected that, by the year 2011, Canada will face a shortage of 113,000 nurses." As Picard also points out, "the number of places in nursing schools is clearly inadequate." All this adds up to a recipe for an overworked, demoralized profession. Picard tells us that "nurses take 50 per cent more sick days than the average worker. They have above-average drug- and alcohol-abuse rates. Their stress levels are through the roof." Restructuring and the staff cutbacks have come on top of years of undervaluing our nurses, who are, not surprisingly, still mostly women. The effect on nurses and on the system has been profound.

We may value our physicians, especially our family doctors, more than our nurses, but not necessarily enough. For most of us, the family physician remains our main point of contact—the health care bureaucrats call this the "access point"—with the health care system. In a recent Ontario survey, more than 90 per cent of respondents reported that they currently have a general practitioner or family doctor whom they have visited within the past two years. The figures are similar across the land. Canada today has one of the highest proportions of family doctors in the world. Roughly 40 per cent of our physicians practise family medicine. Compare this with the proportion in the United States, where the figure is close to 18 per cent, and you'll have another reason their system costs so much more than ours. South of the border, high-priced specialists treat many patients who shouldn't be in their offices at all.

Ominously, however, that healthy percentage of family doctors is beginning to slip and the percentage of specialists is beginning to rise. According to the first annual report of the CIHI, published in the spring of 2000, "Over the past six years, there has been an increase in the proportion of specialists and a decrease in the proportion of family doctors. As with nurses, the average age of physicians is climbing." Encouragingly, the CIHI report finds that the doctor drain to the United States is just about balanced by doctors who are entering the country, either returning Canadians or immigrants with medical jobs waiting for them.

Numbers aside, the care delivered by family physicians in Canada has changed during the past twenty-five years, and not necessarily for the better. When I entered family practice back in 1977, doctors were still making house calls, still talked to their patients on the telephone, and could usually be reached on weekends and after hours. Except for the rare group practice that offers after-hours telephone advice, most urban family physicians in Canada now keep nine-to-five office hours, five days a week. When you call the office during non-office hours, more often than not a voice message tells you to head for the local emergency room or walk-in clinic if your problem can't wait until the next day. And this has become the family-practice norm at a time when most other parts of society seem to be moving towards a round-the-clock—"24/7"—world.

But even during office hours, things have changed. Have you noticed, as many Canadians have, that your family doctor doesn't seem to have as much time to chat as he or she used to? Do you wonder why you have to come back into the office to get your test results or a prescription renewed, visits that take less than five minutes but for which you often wait an hour? A large part of the reason for this is simple economics: in real terms, doctors' incomes have been declining fairly steadily thanks to decreasing revenue and rising costs, a topic I look at in more detail in chapter 3.

Because almost all family doctors are paid on a fee-for-service basis, which means they get the same amount whether they spend five minutes or fifty minutes discussing your complaint before they prescribe the medicine, they feel enormous pressure to see a high volume of patients. Due to fee cutbacks, few of them now employ a registered nurse as part of their practices, further hampering their ability to provide the full spectrum of primary care. And doctors don't get paid for offering any advice over the telephone. They either give it for free or charge a user fee. This doesn't make for the best family medicine—or for patients who feel they've been listened to.

As for Canadian specialists, many of them freely admit that, despite our healthy population of general practitioners, specialists see far too many people who don't belong in their offices. Technically, specialists can be seen only through referral from a family doctor or another specialist. However, impatient patients often call up specialists directly, and some specialists agree to see them. They get around the rules by pretending the patient has been referred. I well remember from my own family practice receiving letters from specialists "thanking" me for referring one of my patients, when, in fact, the patient had referred him- or herself. Self-referral to a specialist has now been banned in Ontario.

Even more serious in my view is the lack of communication between family doctors and specialists, and between family doctors and hospitals. This lack of communication not only costs us a lot of money, but can make for some very bad medicine. For example, if you arrive at the hospital emergency room complaining of chest pains, the admitting physician has no access to your history and there is no expectation that he or she should. Logically, the admitting physician should have immediate access to your most recent cardiogram, if you've had one. By comparing this to your current cardiogram, the doctor can immediately tell whether you've suffered heart damage. If he or she doesn't have access to this information, more tests and more time are needed. The result: bad communication and bad medicine that stem in large part from a system that is not set up to encourage information sharing or investments in information systems.

Failures in communication originate on both sides of the relationship. But I can't tell you how frustrating it is for a family doctor to receive the hospital discharge summary for one of her patients *three months* after the patient has been released from hospital. That's right, three months. Sounds ridiculous, yet it happened to me time after time. Under our current set-up, there is no requirement for hospitals to immediately and automatically inform a person's primary-care physician what drugs he or she is taking and exactly what care took place in the hospital setting. More evidence of the patchwork nature of our current system. As David Naylor, dean of medicine at the University of Toronto, put it in a recent paper, "The way the health care system is organized tends to impede links among institutions and sectors."

Communication with other health care professionals also leaves a lot to be desired. According to Steve Long, a pharmacist with the Calgary Regional Health Authority, the shifting of intravenous drug therapy from hospitals to homes has done more than save on hospital beds. "Often the patient's family physician and community pharmacist were not aware that the patient had received intravenous therapy until the course was complete. This type of practice fragments the patient's medication profile and can complicate the patient–pharmacist and patient–family physician relationship." What could be more ridiculous than your family doctor not knowing what the surgeon who just released you from the hospital prescribed? Yet it happens every day in the Canadian system.

As Long argues, pharmacists are highly trained professionals who ought to be integrated into the treatment loop. Yet, under our current system, they often have little or no direct contact with the physician prescribing the drug they are dispensing, whether that physician is working inside a hospital or in a family practice. And because the three greatest medical solitudes—family doctors, specialists, and hospitals—don't automatically share treatment information with one another, let alone with the pharmacist, pharmacists often don't realize they are dispensing drugs that could actually cause problems.

Long cites a statistic that will surely shock you as much as it did me when I first read it in the article he contributed to the Healthcare *Papers*, a 1999 discussion of primary-care reform published by the *Ontario Hospital Quarterly*: "Drug-related morbidity and mortality has been estimated to cost $76.6 billion a year in ambulatory care settings (treatment that doesn't require a hospital stay) in the United States . . . The cost of non-compliance and inappropriate use of prescription medication in Canada has been estimated at over $7 billion per year . . . This suggests that non-compliance is one of Canada's most expensive disease categories, and that the cost of non-compliance and inappropriate use of prescription medications is similar to the total expenditure on prescription drugs and medical services in Canada." In other words, as many Canadians get sick from the drugs they're taking as are helped by them. And these negative side effects cost our health care system $7 billion each and every year.

Canadians take far too many prescription drugs. We now spend more money on drugs than on doctoring. Here are the figures. While the amount of money spent on hospitals continues to drop—from 42.5 per cent of total health expenditures in 1979 to a projected 31.6 per cent in 1999—drug costs have almost doubled—from 8.6 to 15.2 per cent, more than a full percentage point above our expenditure on physician services (13.9 per cent). In 1997, the last year for which detailed figures are available, Canadians spent $11.3 billion on prescription drugs, up 10 per cent from the year before. Too many of these drugs were completely unnecessary, inappropriately prescribed, or not taken properly. I find it ironic that, for example, Canada is a big supporter of the Direct Observation Therapy (DOT) program in the fight against tuberculosis in the developing world, but doesn't use this method at home. DOT ensures that patients take the drugs they need until the disease is eliminated. This helps explain why we have not yet won the battle against TB in Canada.

Another huge waste of health care dollars and human health comes in the form of unnecessary medical procedures. Evidence gathered in Ontario clinical trials over the past twenty years documents a startling variation in the frequency of some medical procedures. Take hysterectomies, for example. In some parts of the province more than three times the number of women were having their uteruses removed than in others. Or look at the occurrence of Caesarean sections. Once again, the statistics show wild variations by region.

Ellen Hodnett is a professor of nursing at the University of Toronto, a researcher in the Centre for Research in Women's Health, and the first woman and first non-physician to chair the prestigious Clinical Trials Committee of the Medical Research Council of Canada. After conducting a study of C-section frequency in Ontario, Hodnett found that the reason for the variation is as old as doctoring: medicine practised by rote rather than on the latest evidence. She vividly remembers a conversation she had in the early 1990s with the chief of obstetrics in a major Ontario hospital. She asked him what advice he would give to his residents. He replied, "If you want to know what to do, go to the guy who's been in practice for twenty years and ask him." Experience is important, but so is clinical evidence.

Any analysis of the state of Canadian medicare today must include the several government-sanctioned alternatives to the three traditional deliverers of treatment: family doctors, outside specialists, and hospitals. These alternatives include government-funded community health clinics, home care services, and privately owned walk-in clinics.

The walk-in clinic is Canadian health care at its most wasteful. The doctors and nurses who work in these clinics are undoubtedly competent, but the circumstances in which they work make it difficult to be effective. A look at the billing records of a typical walk-in clinic reveals the problem: 90 per cent of the medical problems that walk into these clinics are either non-problems (the common cold) or so complex that they are beyond the clinic's treatment capability (for example, fatigue). Typically, for anything but the most basic complaint, these clinics simply bill the government for their consultation and refer the patient to a hospital or a specialist, having ordered loads of tests along the way. There is rarely follow-up unless the patient insists on it. The waste in health care dollars is enormous. The privately owned clinics make a nice tidy profit for their owners and they cost the system a great deal of money. But as long as some Canadians don't have a family doctor, walk-in clinics will be there to stop the gap. And as long as most people receive no after-hours care or telephone advice from their own family doctors, they will still "walk in"!

Completing this portrait of Canadian health care at the turn of the millennium are two of the pillars of care in the community: home care and chronic long-term care, including nursing homes. According to all the health care economists and health policy analysts, home care is the wave of the future. Well, home care is inexcusable in its present form. In Ontario, for example, for an AIDS patient or a cancer patient who wants to die at home to qualify for twenty-four-hour home care, he or she must promise to die within no more than three months—that's the maximum allowable home care allotment for any individual. In other words, home care—often the most cost-effective way of delivering health care—is being rationed.

Dealing with the issue of the consistency of quality in chronic care facilities and nursing homes is a major problem. (Nursing home standards monitored by regular inspection seem to be among the casualties of recent government cutbacks.) Funding is now geared to the type of institution instead of the level of care a patient requires. There are many good international models for determining how much care different patient populations need, and we could be using them now in Canada. Surely, preventing bedsores, malnutrition and flu epidemics is more cost-effective than dumping countless of our fragile elderly into ambulances that take them to emergency wards, where they often become confused and sicker. Doris Grinspun, executive director of the Registered Nurses Association of Ontario (RNAO), has suggested that nurse practitioners be available in nursing homes for clinical assessment of fevers, rashes, and other common complaints. These professionals would provide appropriate care on-site for many problems that now mean a visit to the hospital. The process would not only be cost-effective, but kinder. It's ironic that we call these institutions nursing homes when all too often there is no nurse available.

To hear stories of vulnerable seniors living at home being told that they are *allowed* only three hours of care but that the home care coordinator thinks they *need* six hours—and this can be arranged if they are willing to pay—is unconscionable. We must be able to provide what is "needed." If people *want* to have more than the professionals think they need, then it is appropriate that they pay. Indeed, this is part of the challenge: to design a fair system that determines the difference between "needs" and "wants." And the decisions about drawing these lines must involve everyone, not just the experts.

If Canadian health care possessed anything resembling a system of accountabilty for both care providers and care recipients, the vast majority of horror stories simply couldn't happen. Medicine is a high-risk business, but there is no way there should be as many mistakes in the system as there are now. An article in the December 1999 issue of the *British Medical Journal* cited a shocking statistic about medical error in America: it rated the frequency of serious medical error resulting in unnecessary illness or death at one for every 100,000 patients. In other words, if the health care system were a major airline, a 747 would be falling out of the sky every week. (While Canada may have a far more efficient and more universal system than the United States, our level of accountability is just as low.) Such a lack of accountability isn't acceptable in the air industry. Why should it be tolerable in the health care business?

To sum up, Canada's health care system is under serious

stress; it is not living up to its mandate and is falling far short of its potential. There has been a great deal of thoughtless tinkering, and very little attempt at comprehensive, system-wide reform. Medicare is not yet in danger of breaking down, but it is failing us more often than it should.

The real crisis: confidence

To my mind, the real crisis in Canadian health care is a crisis of confidence. If Canadians stop believing in their health care system, then no politician will be able to save it. On the other hand, as long as Canadians continue to feel proud of their system and confident that it can continue to serve them well, the system will survive and prosper.

In early 2000, public-opinion polls revealed a fascinating split in the way Canadians viewed the state of medicare. On the one hand, as Angus Reid reported in February, eight in ten Canadians believed that their health care system was in crisis. Another poll reported that 80 per cent of Canadians described their personal health care experience as either "satisfactory" or "excellent" while simultaneously believing the system was "in crisis."

The first annual CIHI report described this contradictory situation as follows: "Some public opinion polls have shown a decline in satisfaction with the health care system as a whole . . . At the same time, Canadians tend to give higher ratings to the care that they personally receive." But as demographer David Foot points out in *Boom, Bust & Echo 2000*, Canadians' faith in their system and its providers won't survive if it doesn't change to meet the needs of an aging population. (The peak of the baby boom generation will be in its seventies, twenty years from now, placing an unprece-dented burden on Canadian medicare.) "The boomers have grown accustomed to a retail environment in which quality products and services are demanded and delivered faster than ever before," says Foot. "If the public system doesn't give them what they want, they will demand the right to buy it for themselves." In short, if we don't fix our public system, we'll have a two-tier system, whether we want it or not.

Canadians still believe profoundly in the principles on which our health care system is based. They rank health care as their number one priority, even over tax relief. But they need to see their politicians moving to fix the system, rather than simply arguing over more money. As Richard Gwyn wrote in a recent *Toronto Star* column, "while our health care system needs to be reformed, it doesn't need to be transformed" into an American-style, two-tier system. Our system is simply too good and too important to us to let it go down the drain without a fight.

A vision for the future

Here's the kind of system I believe we can have if we're willing to fight for it. I envision a patient-centred system in which all levels of care and all types of care are fully integrated, but all care starts and ends where it belongs: with the patient and his or her family physician. An integrated system means the most appropriate provider delivers the optimum care at the best possible price. It means that excellent communication between doctors and their patients is matched by excellent communication among all health care providers, whether nursing homes, community clinics, pharmacists, physiotherapists, specialists, midwives, acute-care hospitals, nurse practitioners, or family doctors.

Such a system would stop blaming doctors and nurses and patients for the problems we've been having and instead create a set of strong incentives to improve health care performance and introduce a system-wide culture of accountability. No longer would doctors and other health care professionals live in fear of making mistakes. Instead, they would be highly motivated to learn from their mistakes—as is already the case in many other industries.

A reformed health care system would quickly move to take advantage of the latest in information technology so that patient records are instantly available when needed and tests won't be repeated or drugs erroneously prescribed for simple lack of information. Technology will also foster more knowledgeable patients, consumers of health care who know good medicine and good care and are prepared to insist on it.

I also envision a system that is truly universal, where no one has to decide whether to pay the rent or pay for prescription drugs or dental care or home care. Such a system need not cost the moon. We will need more money right now for up-front costs, particularly the cost of implementing new information technology and creating a true system of medical accountability. But once these crucial investments have been made, I have no doubt that we can have an optimal public system that would rival any private system with a lot less than the 14.1 per cent of the GDP that the Americans are spending. It may well be more than the 9.3 per cent that we're spending now, but it's up to Canadians to decide how much health care they're prepared to pay for.

Such a system is not an impossible dream, but it won't be achieved by thoughtless tinkering or by simply throwing more money at health care problems. It will be achieved only through comprehensive, system-wide reform, by doctors and nurses and pharmacists and physiotherapists and all the providers of health care working as a team with the patient as the undisputed captain.

Part Two

The Doctor

3

Don't Blame the Doctor

Some personal history

Sir William Osler was, in his day, the most famous physician in the world, a renowned medical educator who revolutionized physician training by actually insisting that medical students examine patients as part of their training. Osler believed that "it is a safe rule . . . that the best teaching is that taught by the patient himself." We would do well to remember Osler's advice.

I often say that I learned as much about the practice of medicine from my patients as from all my teachers in medical school. I still remember two clinical examinations during my training at Toronto General Hospital with a particularly intimidating professor of internal medicine. The first involved a patient with malaria, a man who'd lived in Africa for ten years. The patient knew far more about the disease than I did: how he'd gotten it, why he'd gotten it, and what drugs he should have taken to prevent it. When I presented his case to my professor, I was an expert. I looked really good.

The second patient was a heroin-addicted prostitute with hepatitis B who gave me a seminar in her disease. She explained the difference between hep A and hep B, the different incubation periods, and so on. Once again, when it came time to present her case, the professor was impressed. And so was I, but for a very different reason. I recognized that I had had the most important lesson of all: listen to your patients.

The importance of listening to your patients was first taught me by a wonderful physician whom I met on my very first day of pre-meds at the University of Toronto in the fall of 1968. Her name was Dr. Vera Peters, and her daughter Jenny was one of my classmates. Jenny invited me home after classes that day to meet her mom. I couldn't believe my luck. I already knew Dr. Peters by reputation, as one of the country's leading radiation oncologists. She was an amazing researcher, an international authority on Hodgkin's disease, revered by staff and patients alike at Princess Margaret Hospital.

When I met her that afternoon, I immediately understood why she was such a popular and successful doctor. She asked me probing questions, then listened to my answers and responded with empathy and understanding. She taught me two essential skills for my chosen career: how to drink coffee and how to listen to patients. The secret to this second skill was asking the open-ended question that allows patients to tell you the secret thing that's really worrying them. Quite often, as I would learn, this proves to be the key missing piece to a diagnostic puzzle. I became so accustomed to listening in this open-ended way that I would later have a patient affectionately accuse me of having the word SPILL tattooed on my forehead. Thank you, Dr. Peters.

My ultimate training in the art of listening began in 1977, after I set up a joint family practice in the Annex area of Toronto with my friend and classmate Dr. Jean Marmoreo. Previously a nurse and then a psychotherapist at the Clarke Institute, Jean had a charismatic style and a growing reputation that attracted a discerning group of patients, primarily women. Luckily I became the physician of the new patients her practice didn't have room for.

These women patients comprised an amazing group of people. I swear that every one of them arrived in our waiting room bearing a copy of *Our Bodies, Our Selves*, the self-help book originally published by the Boston Women's Collective in 1969, which by 1977 had become one of the primary texts of the feminist movement. These women patients knew what they wanted. One of those things was to be in control.

They started with an assumption that is almost as revolutionary now as it was then: the patient knows her body best. They arrived armed with knowledge and asked very smart questions about their symptoms. Usually they had already correctly diagnosed the problem and simply wanted me to prescribe the best treatment. Frequently they knew what the best treatment was. They didn't call me up complaining of increased urination and a burning sensation while urinating, they called up to demand a sulpha prescription for their bladder infection—now! On other occasions, if I prescribed a course of treatment, they wanted to know the evidence supporting it. When there was no good answer, they weren't satisfied.

Among my patients were several heavy smokers with recurrent bronchitis. (I'd done my best to talk them into quitting, to no avail.) These patients were capable of diagnosing themselves in certain situations and I let them do it. At the beginning of each winter season I would write them a prescription and trust them to fill it if they needed it. They knew that if their sputum turned green or they developed a fever that their bronchitis had recurred and they needed to fill their prescription. Of course, this kind of family medicine means knowing your patients and having an ongoing, trusting relationship with them.

My women patients educated me on the subject of childbirth, which I considered one of my specialties. They didn't
buy the prevailing attitude that childbirth was a disaster
waiting to happen. They pointed out that many of the rules
for childbirth seemed to be designed for the convenience of
doctors, rather than for the needs of pregnant women. They
hired midwives and labour coaches, non-physicians who
taught me much about the practice of obstetrics. No question, each of those well-informed, demanding, and sometimes difficult women was the boss!

Those early years, as our practice grew, and as my
patients challenged me on a daily basis, taught me to be a
better doctor. My learning continued when Jean Marmoreo
and I joined a larger practice, the Bedford Medical Group.
In 1983 we teamed up with a number of doctors we'd
come to know through our association with Women's
College Hospital, all of them family physicians with a
special interest in obstetrics. At Bedford Medical we shared
one belief: we could deliver better, more comprehensive
care to our patients practising together than we could practising alone or in very small partnerships.

The early days at Bedford Medical will probably remain
my peak experience of practising medicine. Our practice
was "on call" pretty much all the time. When a patient
phoned up our answering service, the service would automatically page whoever was on call that particular evening
or weekend. Once our practice reached eight doctors, we
could spread out the overtime. Each of us was on call one
weekday evening every other week and on weekend call—
from Friday evening to Monday morning—every eighth
weekend. Weekend call, from Friday evening to Monday
morning, included staffing the Saturday clinic.

In those days, we made house calls and took on patients

who needed palliative care. We had wonderful nurses on staff who could handle a host of ordinary complaints, both medical and psychological. We also provided after-hours telephone advice, lots of it. My husband, Peter, used to joke that I should wear a coin dispenser so that I would always have quarters handy when I was on call. Those were the days before cell phones, so when my beeper went I needed three quarters: one to call the answering service and pick up the message; one to call the patient and discuss the problem; and often one more to call the pharmacy with a prescription. I also dispensed telephone advice during office hours—anything to give me more time with the patients who really needed to see me. I believe that in those days we really ran a patient-centred group practice, one that was in many ways a model of what should be not only possible, but normal in our health care system.

Why don't such group practices abound and flourish? The sad answer is that the system isn't set up to encourage them.

"Those greedy doctors"

Last April, the Toronto papers trumpeted the revelation that the highest paid family physicians in Ontario were billing at a rate that meant they had to be seeing more than eighty patients a day. A month earlier, twelve doctors from a Mississauga walk-in clinic were charged with fraud. The Ontario Provincial Police had evidence the clinic had charged OHIP $2 million during 1997 for services the clinic had not performed.

With these types of stories making headlines, it's all too easy to blame "those greedy doctors" for many of the problems in our health care system. But to do so misses the point and avoids getting at root causes. I don't believe that most doctors are consciously trying to maximize their incomes by minimizing the time they spend with patients. The solo practitioners who bill for more patients in a single day than any human doctor could possibly see are another story. We can't blame doctors for all the rising costs and declining satisfaction. But we can place considerable blame on the way most doctors are paid: the fee-for-service model.

The way our fee-for-service payment system has evolved, it now promotes bad medicine. It has led to what one prominent family practitioner has called "rampant incompetence." George Pink, a professor of health administration at the University of Toronto, refers to fee-for-service as one of our system's "perverse incentives," since under it "everybody has the incentive to do volume. And nobody has the incentive to do only what's necessary or what's right." The fee-for-service model rewards quantity not quality. Here's how fee-for-service works.

Each service a doctor performs has a price set out in the provincial fee schedule, which is a binder of loose-leaf pages covered with fine print that is regularly modified and updated through consultations and negotiations between the Health ministry and representatives of the medical profession. A family doctor charges a set amount based on the type of consultation each time he or she sees a patient, regardless of how long he or she spends. Likewise, a specialist can charge only a set amount for each service provided. A surgeon receives more for removing an appendix than for excising an infected cyst, but earns the same amount whether the pre-operative consultation takes five minutes or fifty. Whether you are a family doctor or a radiation oncologist or a specialist in geriatrics, the government pays you according to the fee schedule only up to a set annual limit. In Ontario, for example, the government reimburses the doctor for only 25 per cent of the scheduled fee beyond this ceiling.

There's a big chunk of some doctors' incomes, however, that doesn't come from the government, but out of the patient's pocket. These are the fees doctors charge for services that have been delisted from the fee schedule and so are no longer covered. Delisted items vary from province to province, but they have in some cases opened up lucrative areas of privatized medicine, for example, laser surgery and plastic surgery and the removal of a non-infected cyst. In this embryonic but growing private system, patients pay what the market will bear. The latest deal between the Ontario government and the Ontario Medical Association, which increases the number of delisted services, is part of a worrisome trend that, if allowed to continue, will lead to *de facto* two-tier medicine in Canada. I believe it is no longer appropriate for decisions such as delisting to be made behind closed doors by two parties (government and doctors) who both receive financial benefit from the decision. Citizens must be at the table to define what is "medically necessary."

The recent debate in Alberta over "enhanced" services has highlighted the conflict that arises when the decision to "delist" or "not list" can be made for ideological reasons. The Alberta government believes that privatization is good and that it will be good for medicare if more doctors can charge for certain high-demand services. Many Albertans are not happy about this trend.

Of greater immediate concern, however, is the way the fee-for-service system encourages "practice churning," a situation where doctors try to move as many patients as possible through their offices each day and to bring them back as often as possible, so they can bill for another consultation. This is what is really going on when your doctor refuses to do a PAP smear as part of your annual check-up, telling you it's "our policy" to see you in three weeks to discuss your test results, at which time a PAP smear will be done separately. Patients should be outraged when their doctors play this kind of creative billing game that places no value on patients' time.

Fee-for-service penalizes the family doctors who actually take the time to listen to their patients or explain a diagnosis until the patient understands. It penalizes some specialists—gerontology specialists, for example, whose patients require more time per consultation than do, say, those of dermatologists. Whether you are a specialist or a general practitioner in Canada, the more time you spend with each patient, the less money you make. Fee schedules have never set a high enough—or even adequate—value on doctor–patient communication or on certain types of "soft" services doctors render.

I well remember when I started practice in Toronto after a brief stint practising in Midland, Ontario. My Midland medical friends couldn't believe I could spend a whole day seeing twenty to twenty-five patients—the average in Midland was at least double. I tried to explain that an urban practice is different from one in a smaller centre, and that I couldn't have done my job properly and seen any more. Fee-for-service leaves many doctors feeling the fee system is unfair and many many patients feeling shortchanged by their doctors.

A recent survey of the medical profession conducted for the *Journal of the American Medical Association* reported the following amazing responses from Canadian and U.S. physicians:

- Average number of seconds a doctor waits before interrupting a patient's description of the problem? 18 seconds.

- Average number of seconds a patient spends describing his or her problem when not being interrupted? 90 seconds.
- Percentage of patients' concerns about their problems that are not elicited by doctors? 45 per cent.
- Percentage of psychosocial and psychiatric problems that are missed by doctors? 50 per cent.

Think for a moment about what these answers mean. You've got only eighteen seconds to state your case before the doctor takes over! Even the doctors themselves know this isn't enough time to hear you out properly. Yet they feel such pressure to move you through their offices that they won't give you even the minute and a half you need. As a result, doctors will admit they're missing almost as many problems as they catch. No wonder patient surveys consistently show that the most common complaint people have about their physicians is lack of information and lack of communication.

A recent analysis found that 67 per cent of complaints to the College of Physicians and Surgeons of Ontario, the body that polices the medical profession, are related to poor communication rather than medical mistakes. A recent poll sponsored by Women's College Hospital found that 40 per cent of women patients had switched doctors because they weren't satisfied with the quality of treatment or the level of service, and 25 per cent had sought a second opinion without telling their own doctor. In 1995, Women's College Hospital sponsored a nationwide survey of women's attitudes towards health; the survey found that 55 per cent of women's dissatisfaction with their health care derived from their doctors' attitudes.

The vast majority of physicians want to practise good medicine and are trying to do so under ever more difficult circumstances. They certainly didn't enter the profession because they wanted to become fabulously rich. They haven't forgotten the Hippocratic oath. They want to help people, to make their lives better. They want to feel good about themselves and their jobs.

What's up, Doc?

I'd say that the morale of Canadian physicians has never been lower. They believe that what they are doing is important, but they feel it is undervalued. At the most basic and most selfish level, they feel underpaid—with some reason. Doctors are "virtual" civil servants: they get paid by the government but they don't get the benefits of government employees: the pensions, vacation pay, or paid time off for further education that comes attached to a civil-service job.

Doctors' real incomes have dropped from four times the national average in 1970 to 3.4 times the national average in 1990 and 1995. Between 1980 and 1995, the overall earnings of physicians declined 2 per cent because of the extraordinary growth in the number of young female physicians. Male physicians moved from an average of $116,100 to $117,200. Real average earnings of female physicians increased by 19 per cent from $63,600 to $76,000.

Compared with other professionals, including the hospital CEOs pulling in upwards of $500,000, many doctors see themselves as falling behind. (Because only doctors' gross billing statistics are published, many people believe that most physicians are making at least $200,000 a year. Once rent, employee salaries, professional dues, malpractice insurance, and all other expenses are subtracted, most make much less.) But they still have the same mortgages, the same living expenses. Their gross incomes are capped, they've cut their office overhead to the bone, laid off their nurses and nurse practitioners. Yet within specialties with high operating costs that can't easily be cut, some doctors are facing bankruptcy, a fate far different from the financial comfort they expected would repay their years of training at a modest wage. No wonder many are succumbing to the lure of American medicine, where doctors can become very wealthy indeed.

In a talk I gave a few years ago to the Ontario College of Family Physicians, I put up a slide of Eeyore, the perpetually pessimistic donkey in A.A. Milne's *Winnie the Pooh*. Eeyore's motto was "Nobody minds, nobody cares." That's exactly the way Canadian family doctors feel these days. In my specialty, family medicine, doctors are finding it harder and harder to do the kind of job they would like to do. Patients generally have high regard for their own doctors but often express cynicism about the profession as a whole.

A recent survey of Ontario family physicians by the Ontario College of Family Medicine found that fully 80 per cent "agreed that it is increasingly difficult to practise according to the four principles of family medicine," which are:

- The patient–physician relationship is central to the role of the family physician.
- The family physician is a skilled clinician.
- The family physician is a resource to a defined practice population.
- Family medicine is a community-based discipline.

These may seem obvious statements, but in the current health care universe they are closer to messages from

45

another planet. My conversations with family doctors across the country confirm that this crucial 40 per cent of all practitioners, the family physicians at the forefront of primary care, are disillusioned and increasingly demoralized. And they are afraid that primary-care reforms being proposed by governments will make their jobs even harder, forcing them to see more patients, work longer hours, spend money they don't have on expensive technology, and earn less.

I recently received an eloquent and heartfelt letter from Dr. Julie McIntyre, a very fine family physician who practises in my riding of St. Paul's in midtown Toronto. While she applauded my desire to see a more modern, integrated system she's afraid that the proposed reforms will make things worse for many doctors and for many patients. Because I believe she expresses both the idealism and the genuine fears of many solo practitioners, I have asked her to let me reproduce part of her letter in this book. She writes:

What seems to be lost in all the debate about our health care system is the impact of all this on our human interactions and our sense of security and well-being. A good family physician, in the right work environment, can make a patient feel like there is someone . . . who truly cares about them on a personal level and will be an advocate for them. The sense of well-being this can promote cannot be exaggerated—the effect across the population can be enormous.

In order to provide this type of care, the family physician needs:

• Access to specialists, diagnostic tests, home care support, emergency and hospital services in a timely manner (in addition to communication and reports from same).

- Relative freedom from financial pressures. (I don't mean I need a BMW; I do mean I don't want to have to worry about being able to pay the rent. Many don't realize that the OHIP fee schedule pays us only about half of what our professional association has determined our services to be worth. To be paid the difference would be considered "extra-billing.")

- A manageable number of patients to care for. I have a relatively small practice of about 900 patients, many seniors, and work about 4½ days/week. I see approximately 20 patients/day and still usually feel rushed and rarely get home before 8 p.m. If I had a family to support or no spouse to share household expenses, I could not afford to practise in this way. I know that most of my colleagues need to see far more patients in order to survive financially and also, in areas of physician shortages (which includes parts of Toronto), to meet patient demand. This problem will increase as the population grows and family physician numbers dwindle, i.e., as more retire, sub-specialize, or move to avoid the increasingly difficult work environment. Already, a large proportion of Canadian Family Practice graduates, considered among the best trained in the world, choose to leave Canada!

- Time to update skills and knowledge (including becoming computer-literate).

- Time for family, friends, exercise, relaxation, and reflection.

I believe that most of us who practise family medicine feel incredibly lucky to have a profession which allows us the privilege to become as close as we do to our patients and to be able to provide valuable help to those people we truly care for. A system that allows us to do this will have immeasurable long-term benefits in terms of both health care and economic outcomes.

The Doctor

I don't believe this doctor's fears will come true, not if we reform the system well, but her fears are shared by many and they must be listened to. I agree with everything she has to say about how physicians should be able to practise. I believe the reforms I outline in Part Four of this book will make it possible for more doctors to practise medicine the way it should be practised. But first we'll have to take down one of the barriers to effective doctoring: the unnecessary gulf between family physicians and specialists.

Don't blame the specialists

When family doctors get together, there are certain things they always complain about. One of these things is the way they are treated by specialists, who make up more than 50 per cent of Canadian physicians. A recent editorial in the *Medical Post* summed up the situation aptly: "Unfortunately, in many provinces GPs don't trust specialists and specialists have little faith in the leadership of GPs."

I'm sure when groups of specialists get together to commiserate, they say pretty much the same thing about family doctors. Many specialists will tell you that a patient's primary-care physician is often guilty of not providing the necessary information to ensure proper treatment or of simply dumping a difficult patient into a specialist's lap rather than dealing with the real problem. They will point out that many specialists do a superb job of working with general practitioners—I've referred my patients to many of them! These doctors really believe in coordinated integrated care.

Like general practitioners, many doctors who work in specialized disciplines are feeling the pinch of fee caps, cutbacks, and hospital restructuring. Worst off are the specialists who toil inside hospitals. Like our acute-care nurses, they are dealing with a much more difficult work environment than a few years ago. Fewer support staff, too few beds, reduced facilities, and a higher than ever pressure to move their patients out of those precious hospital beds have increased the stress load of hospital physicians. They bear the brunt of criticism patients level at hospitals. They are working as hard as ever, but many of them are earning less money.

General surgeons, in particular, are feeling the pinch. In the many hospitals that have been downsized or amalgamated, where operating rooms have been closed and access to operating facilities has been reduced for elective surgery, many surgeons find themselves with too little income-generating activity. Yet they still have to be on call for emergencies. I know of some fine surgeons who support themselves doing routine operations that seem a waste of their talents. For example, I know of one surgeon, an expert in head and neck cancers, who spends most of his time performing uvulectomies, a simple operation to alleviate heavy snoring. Like most other doctors in Canada, surgeons earn a fee for service. When they look at the fees other specialists are earning, the system looks unjust to them as well. They are not alone.

The "procedure" specialists, such as dermatologists and gastro-enterologists, are doing very well. The "talking" specialists, such as psychiatrists, are falling behind. There is a finite number of fifty-minute hours in any given week. Obstetricians, whose lifestyles are at the mercy of the baby delivery schedule, can be on call twenty-four hours a day, yet earn less than one-tenth the income of their American colleagues while also paying higher premiums for malpractice insurance than other specialists. These doctors are sorely tempted to move south or move over to the less exhausting and more lucrative practice of gynecology.

The Doctor

Those specialists who spend time teaching, who volunteer to serve on committees, who continuously upgrade their skills and knowledge, or who undertake essential medical research suffer in comparison to their colleagues who choose a nine-to-five private practice filled with lucrative procedures.

Let's not blame all specialists for the problems with Canadian health care. Most specialists, like most family physicians, work hard to deliver the best care possible. Most are highly skilled and dedicated to their jobs. But they are operating in an increasingly difficult environment, one that amplifies the divisions and jealousies among specialties and that doesn't promote cooperation between the primary care delivered by family doctors and the care delivered by specialists.

Don't blame the specialists, blame the system.

Too few doctors?

One of the commonest criticisms you hear about Canadian medicare is that many communities have too few doctors, while other places, big cities for the most part, are over-supplied. Some argue that, even if the physician population were better distributed, Canada would have too few doctors. The Canadian Medical Association certainly thinks so. Its 1999 task force report, *Physician Supply in Canada*, noted that since 1992 the country's medical schools have been turning out fewer doctors—the result of a 1991 study that predicted oversupply and called for a 10 per cent reduction in medical students—while Canada's population has continued to grow. As a result, the annual input of newly trained doctors into the system is lower than it was in 1974, while our population has risen from 22 million to 30.5 million.

According to the CMA task force, "physician shortages are reported in urban as well as rural and remote areas.

Many specialties are reporting shortages (e.g., Anesthesia, Psychiatry, Radiology, Obstetrics, Radiation Oncology), and physican morale is low. Waiting lists have grown."

However, if you look at the number of physicians per 100,000 of population, Canada compares very favourably with other countries: We have 221 to the Americans' 245, while Great Britain has 164, Japan 177, Sweden 299, and Cuba 518! Compared to the United States, Canada has a much higher proportion of family physicians. In the United States, all primary-care physicians (family physicians, general internists, general pediatricians, and obstetricians) are lumped together and represent from 25 per cent to 30 per cent of all medical practitioners. American family physicians comprise a mere 18 per cent of all MDs. Good studies have shown that the best health care systems have a 50/50 ratio of family physicians to specialists. As Cal Gutkin, executive director of the College of Family Physicians of Canada, explains, "The ratio of family practitioners to specialists in Canada has fallen below 50/50 because of a relative drop in new family practice post-grad slots since 1992 (compared to specialty training slots) and because of a relatively greater outmigration of family practitioners compared to specialists, mainly to the United States over the past decade. The ratio in training programs, which was also 50/50 at one time, has dropped to 38/62. We need more family practice training slots and more family practitioners in practice."

Yes, we certainly must start turning out greater numbers of well-trained doctors and we must introduce strong incentives for them to stay in Canada. We may indeed need more doctors, but we definitely need to address the problem of maldistribution.

In many parts of Canada, the too few doctors are trying to look after too many patients, putting them under enormous pressure just to serve their existing patient populations and making them unable to take new patients. There are some large communities in this country, for example, Thunder Bay, Ontario, where thousands of residents go without a family doctor because the local family physicians are stretched to the limit. This situation places even more stress on hospital emergency rooms and increases the demand for walk-in clinics. The lack of continuity that comes with getting one's primary care in emergency rooms or clinics has unhealthy side effects. Family physicians are trained to look for problems like spousal abuse, and they are able to detect them because they have ongoing relationships with their patients. Without such ongoing medical involvement, these problems often go unnoticed and unreported. Subtler medical conditions, like some cancers that can be treated if detected in their early stages, are missed. Chronic conditions aren't managed properly. I recently learned of a practice in rural Saskatchewan where one family physician has managed to look after 4,000 patients by hiring three nurse practitioners.

Every Canadian should have access to a family doctor. Every Canadian who is referred to a specialist should be able to see that specialist in a timely fashion. All Canadians need to be reassured that our medical schools are turning out enough doctors to meet our future needs and that the doctor shortages in many regions will be remedied. And we need a coherent policy that welcomes qualified doctors from other countries who want to practise in Canada.

Very worrying is the "greying" of our specialists and subspecialists. Dean Noni MacDonald of Dalhousie Medical School has pointed out that of our thirty-two pediatric nephrologists in Canada (the people who provide kidney dialysis for children), sixteen are now over the age of sixty. The inflexible nature of residency programs must also be changed. Residents in one specialty are not permitted to switch if they decide it's not for them. And there are no post-graduate slots available for family doctors who want to return to school to train in a specialty.

Doctors' dilemma

Recent surveys show that family doctors are increasingly willing to consider alternatives to the fee-for-service model and that they are willing to question the efficacy of solo practitioners working in isolation. Many specialists, increasingly demoralized by the discrepancies in earning power among different disciplines, have expressed a willingness to consider alternatives. Hugh Scully, a respected cardiovascular surgeon who is currently president of the Canadian Medical Association, is on record arguing that his specialty should be put on salary. He can do only so many surgeries per year: Why not just pay him for doing a full-time job and let him get on with his work? Some teaching hospitals have adopted an alternative payment plan for their physician employees. One of these is Toronto's Hospital for Sick Children. Reviews so far are mixed—there are reports of doctors moonlighting to enhance their earnings—but there is nonetheless a growing consensus within the Canadian medical profession in support of changing the way doctors are paid.

Consensus for reform is growing among family physicians. Many family doctors are questioning not just the way family medicine is delivered, but the way the whole health care system is organized. Canadian physicians face a fundamental choice as system-wide health care reform becomes more urgent. They can be part of the problem or part of the solution.

4

The Doctor
Is Part of the Solution

Value shift

Our best doctors, whether general practitioners or specialists, are often at the leading edge of change. Many of
Canada's finest medical minds are grappling with ways to
fix our ailing health care system. Many forward-thinking
physicians are already experimenting with alternative
models of care. We don't hear as much about these pioneers
as we do about the advocates of privatization and Ameri-
canization, but they deserve to be recognized and celebrated. Their research and their front-line experience are
showing the way to better health care for all of us.

At the risk of oversimplifying, I'd say that the progressive
thinkers and doers in Canadian medicine share certain key
ideas and values. They believe our health care system is one
of the main reasons that Canada is such a good country to
live in. They see health care as a multidisciplinary world in
which doctors play an important but collaborative role.
They understand that there must be a focus on prevention
and keeping people healthy. They are skilled clinicians who
believe in what is known as evidence-based practice. They
aren't afraid of alternative approaches and alternative practitioners. Many of them incorporate non-traditional medicine into their practices and some are participating in

research into the potential of alternative therapies such as acupuncture for pain control. Most of all, they like the idea of working as part of a team, both in their own practices and in terms of the way the whole system is organized.

Quite a few of these doctors already work in groups, sharing the workload and striving to provide care for their patients twenty-four hours a day, seven days a week. Some of them are working inside hospitals, endeavouring to reform the way the acute-care sector operates, to integrate this important but relatively small fraction of the health care universe into the whole system of care.

But perhaps the single most important value they share is in the way they look at patients.

Seeing patients as partners

In 1983, I started teaching low-risk obstetrics at Women's College Hospital, which had long been a unique part of the Toronto medical landscape. Women's College began life in the late nineteenth century as a medical college for women during the era of separate-but-not-equal education for women doctors. When the college was absorbed into the University of Toronto, its dispensary became the foundation of what emerged as Women's College Hospital.

By the time I was learning how to practise family medicine from the highly informed women patients in my private practice, Women's College had become a beacon of progressive, patient-centred medicine in Toronto, in Ontario, and in North America. The attitude I encountered among the staff, whether doctors or nurses or radiation technologists or social workers, might be aptly summed up in the hospital's motto, Non quo, sed quo modo: It's not what you do, but how you do it. The experience of being a patient at Women's College truly was different because the hospital understood that if you pay attention to the process—the way medicine is done—the results, or outcomes, will be better. And they were.

Above all, Women's College was a pioneer in health care for women. Its approach was defined in the following six principles:

1. Empowerment of women, which includes informed, participative decision making, community input, and consumer evaluation of programs.
2. Accessibility of programs through flexible schedules, sensitivity to cultural and linguistic issues, and self-referral to programs as appropriate.
3. Broad definition of health care, including disease-prevention and health-promotion programs, flexible models of care, and the provision of care appropriate to different stages in a woman's life cycle.
4. High quality of care which is compassionate and empathetic, and which acknowledges the choices individuals make based on their own unique experiences and perceptions.
5. Collaborative planning, demonstrated by provision of health care by an interdisciplinary team in conjunction with community partnership.
6. Innovative and creative approaches to women's health-research issues and in response to contemporary health issues.

Reading over these six principles, I'm amazed how well they stand up today. If you substituted the word *people* for the word *women* these six principles would make a solid philosophy on which to base a reform of our whole system of health care. Each and every principle puts the patient at the centre. Again and again there is a sense of people working together—patients and nurses and doctors; doctors and nurses and other health care providers; health care providers and other members of the community. What's more, these principles weren't just written down and filed away in a drawer in the hospital public relations office, they were the living, breathing reality of day-to-day life at Women's College. They put real meaning into that overworked and much abused word empowerment. At Women's College, the patients, both men and women, felt their power.

It's not surprising, therefore, that as soon as I started working at Women's College, I realized it was a place where my patients would feel at home. It was there that my expecting mothers came for the delivery of their babies and there that I referred most of my patients in need of acute care. At Women's College, my patients were given the information they needed in order to take a large share of the responsibility for their treatment. Instead of being passive recipients of health care, they became active participants in their own care.

The Diabetes Education Unit, the Back Education Unit, the Breast Cancer Unit, each of these multidisciplinary units within the hospital structure was designed to give women the information they needed to make informed choices about their treatment. Note the word choices. Care at Women's College was designed to make the patient feel in control of her care. WCH predicated its approach on what was best for patients, not what was most convenient for doctors.

One of the most graphic examples of the Women's College approach came from the hospital's sexual assault–care centre. The head of the centre was a wonderful social worker named Mary Addison who actually listened to her clients, a rare quality among health care providers in those days. What Mary heard from her clients who had just experienced the trauma of sexual assault was that they were in no condition to make reasoned decisions about whether or not to press criminal charges.

In other hospitals, not deciding to press charges at the time of treatment was tantamount to deciding not to lay charges ever, because the samples necessary as evidence were only taken if the woman had decided to lay charges. The sexual assault–care centre at Women's College solved this situation by buying a freezer, where samples could be stored for up to six months, ample time for the victim to make a calm decision. At the time it seemed like a stroke of genius. But then, common sense often does. The Women's College model has now been replicated in thirty centres across Ontario. And all because the staff at one hospital actually listened to the patients.

Another example comes to mind, this one the story of a childbirth with unexpected complications. The mother in question happened to be the daughter-in-law of a prominent physician at nearby Toronto General. I gather this gentleman's nose went somewhat out of joint when she chose to have her baby at Women's College instead of his own institution. The birth went normally, the baby was fine, and the mother and child were discharged after a routine stay of three days.

A few days later, the mother arrived at the Women's College emergency room, with her baby in tow. She was complaining of abdominal pain that presented as probable appendicitis. The emergency room doctor then did two extraordinary things, virtually unheard of in a big city emergency room then or now: (1) she admitted both the mother and her baby; (2) she phoned the woman's obstetrician, the person who had delivered the baby and who knew her best.

The delivering doctor—who could actually be reached right away!—came straight down to the hospital, examined her patient, and then consulted with someone from General Surgery. Together they decided that an appendectomy was warranted. Surgery was scheduled immediately.

Within a few hours of being admitted to the emergency room, the new mother was back in the maternity ward, breast-feeding her baby. Her father-in-law, who'd arrived on the scene as this drama unfolded, commented afterwards: "This place really is different."

The difference was and remains sad but true. At hospitals then, as at hospitals now, the best interests of the patient too often take second place to what's most convenient for the hospital and the doctor. It would have been more convenient and less time-consuming for the emergency room doctor to have simply called in someone from General Surgery who would have ordered the appendectomy without bothering to consult the patient's primary doctor, the one who'd delivered the baby. It would have been more convenient for the surgeon who performed the appendectomy if her patient had recuperated in the surgical ward. But in all ways it was better for the patient—not to mention her newborn baby—to be treated as she was.

I've even heard of patients being bounced back and forth between Toronto hospitals because of silly rivalries over turf. In 1989, when I was part of the fight to save Women's College from being swallowed by the newly amalgamated Toronto Hospital, I brought one such turf war to light. I used this particular example, which I'd been told about by one of the interns involved, in a deputation I made before Toronto City Council. The story went like this.

One day a woman presented herself at the emergency room of Toronto Western Hospital, already part of the newly merged Toronto Hospital. At the Western the emergency room doctors were concerned the woman might be suffering from an ectopic pregnancy, a condition in which the embryo starts to develop somewhere in the fallopian tubes instead of the uterus. Such a tubal pregnancy can cause the fallopian tubes to burst, resulting in heavy internal bleeding. If not operated on promptly, the patient can die.

Unfortunately for this poor woman, the central planners at Toronto Hospital had previously decided that the Western didn't need a gynecologist on staff. Gynecology had been moved in its entirety to the Toronto General. So the doctors at the Western packed the woman into a taxi and sent her over to Toronto General, where a gynecologist examined her, ordered an ultrasound, and concluded the problem was an inflamed appendix.

This is where the story gets unbelievable. Because the doctors at Toronto General didn't want to tread on the toes of the Department of General Surgery at Toronto Western, they packed the woman into a cab and sent her back to the place she'd started from. If ever there was an example of medicine practised at the convenience of doctors, this was it. And if ever there was a reason why women needed a patient-centred hospital like Women's College, this was the reason.

I'm sorry to report that, in Ontario's recently downsized and restructured hospital system, this sort of story is still being told. As my experience at WCH taught me, if more doctors are going to become part of the solution instead of part of the problem, a major attitude shift is needed. Only when more doctors treat their patients as partners—even at the risk of giving up some of their power—will they be drivers of change instead of impediments to change. Fortunately, more and more doctors in Canada are learning to listen better and share the decision-making process with their patients. It can't happen soon enough.

Evidence-based practice

Second only to a shift in the way doctors relate to their patients is the need for the profession to accelerate the shift to evidence-based practice. Contrary to popular belief, the daily practice of family medicine is often a far from scientific activity. A great deal of medical behaviour is still based on the way things have always been done rather than on firm clinical evidence.

I learned this lesson the hard way when I began attending births. Not only did my women patients make me consider alternatives to traditional hospital obstetrics, they wanted the evidence on which these traditional ways of doing things was based. Here are some of the questions they asked me: Why does my labour have to be induced? Why do I have to go to a sterile operating room just to "give birth"? Why can't my mother or my sister—or my husband!—be present at the birth? Why does the fact I've had one Caesarean section mean that all my future babies must be delivered surgically?

In trying to answer these questions I discovered that many of the answers weren't very good. The standard answer was: "Because that's the way it's always been done." The answer behind this response was often: "I'm more comfortable doing things the way I was taught." I soon realized there was little or no evidence to support many traditional obstetrical practices.

I was not alone. For one, Murray Enkin at McMaster University had already begun working with the Cochrane Collaboration in Oxford to determine which childbirth practices were truly "evidence-based." Enkin's work coincided with the rise of the midwifery movement. Some of these pioneering midwives joined forces with Enkin in rigorously examining current practice and delineating what was best for women and their babies during the birthing process. Their work and the work of similar doctors and midwives all over North America reclaimed childbirth as a much more natural phenomenon. As a result, babies are born very differently today.

Acceptance of lumpectomy as the optimal treatment for most breast cancers was extremely slow in coming. Clinicians like Dr. Vera Peters and places like Women's College were much quicker to examine the evidence and opt for an equally effective treatment that didn't require complete breast removal. The evidence indicated that for patients suffering from similar cancers, lumpectomies were just as effective as total mastectomies. Yet for years we kept hearing stories of high-profile American women unnecessarily undergoing this mutilating surgery. Apparently American doctors were afraid of being sued, should the cancer recur, for doing less than the maximum procedure. Rates of lumpectomy versus mastectomy still range widely. But the evidence is clear.

Evidence-based practice means medical practice based on clinical evidence, not on the way things have always been done. It means using the latest clinical research to evaluate all treatments and procedures. Laboratory and clinical research backed up by randomized trials can help us decide where to spend our health care dollars, which test to do when and so on. With cholesterol screening, for example, after two normal tests most people need subsequent screens no more often than once every three years. A Manitoba study suggests that most bladder infections could be treated safely and successfully over the phone, without a culture.

These sorts of examples of more evidence-based practice can also save the system a lot of money.

Nowhere is better evidence more needed than when it comes to the prescription of medication. Prescription drug use in Canada is out of control. Many drugs are prescribed unnecessarily or inappropriately—in part because of the pressure to move patients through the practice. It takes much longer to explain to a patient that he or she doesn't need a prescription for a viral infection than to just write the prescription the patient came in expecting to get. Physicians too often resort to drug treatment before they've tried "lifestyle" treatments, including measures to reduce stress or improve diet. It's a lot easier to put someone on sleeping pills than to figure out what's keeping him or her awake at night. Too many patients are still on old-fashioned drugs for which there are newer and safer substitutes.

Evidence-based practice is based on the latest and the most solid research. Under a system where the doctor is part of the solution, it will be incumbent on every physician, whether in general or specialized practice, to conduct evidence-based practice.

In Canadian family practice, we already have a growing population of such doctors. These are the graduates of the schools of family medicine—in effect, specialists in general practice. As one of these "platinum trained"—that's how the Americans refer to our family-practice graduates—family doctors, I am required to spend a minimum fifty hours a year updating my medical knowledge of and honing my skills in family medicine. Fifty hours isn't onerous. It's the equivalent of one week in the office. Surely such a requirement for continuing education should be made of every physician.

Constantly updating skills is part of what the College of

The Doctor

Family Physicians means when it says all family doctors should be skilled clinicians. Skilled clinicians practise evidence-based medicine growing out of the latest research. They are able to continually change their approach. They don't expect to be able to keep practising the way they did the day they graduated from college. Fortunately, we already have many thousands of such family doctors in Canada. At the present time there are 15,000 members of the College of Family Physicians, which represents between 53 per cent and 62 per cent of all the family physicians in the country. They are a firm foundation on which to build the reformed system. They are part of the solution.

Practising outside the box

Our medical schools also have an important role to play in reforming Canadian health care. After all, they are training the doctors of the future who will be practising in a world where medicine is far more broadly defined than when I was a young intern. No longer can doctors afford to practise inside a box that might be called Sickness Care.

I'd like to see medical schools emphasize some of the following: social determinants of health, including poverty, domestic violence, and environment; doctor–patient relationships; cost-effective quality care; the evidence for non-traditional and alternative health care practices; the role of self-help groups in patient care.

In my own practice I found that self-help groups could make a huge difference for patients dealing with certain types of illnesses, such as cancer. Such groups have proliferated in recent years, and more and more doctors are referring patients to them. This is especially true with chronic illnesses where we doctors, who've been trained to "fix" things, have to admit that we can't fix the illness but perhaps can make the rest of a person's life more liveable. I admit, however, that many physicians stubbornly resist any non-medical referrals. Such doctors are definitely not riding the wave to the future.

Above all, our medical schools need to turn out physicians highly trained in two areas: listening skills and teamwork. In the health care world of the twenty-first century, doctors will need both these skills to operate effectively. The days of solo physicians practising in isolation are numbered. Whether general or specialized, medical practitioners will be part of a team that practises medicine at the convenience of, and by listening to, the patient.

I can easily imagine a medical education model that brings together the different providers in team training sessions. Nurses, whose education puts much more emphasis on teamwork, could thus help train doctors in this vital skill. Team training and learning to listen should be pre-requisites of every medical degree. Pharmacy students and doctors learn the same pharmacology. Maybe if medical students and pharmacy students attended the same classes, doctors would have more respect for what pharmacists know. I can think of all sorts of other examples: physiotherapists learn the same anatomy; social workers learn the same basic psychosocial skills. Increasing our knowledge of what other health care professionals know and what they do will make for a better, more respectful working relationship. The new wave of "problem-based learning" is perfect for this kind of multidisciplinary training.

Team doctors

Many of the doctors who are part of the solution are already practising in group settings. This is particularly true for family practitioners. Despite the prevailing image that most family doctors practise alone or in very small partnerships, a surprising number are joining forces—and not just to save on overhead! A January 1999 survey of Ontario family physicians found that 58 per cent were already working in some sort of group practice.

We hope that those group practices that aren't already doing so will move towards offering their services twenty-four hours a day, seven days a week, and begin to make house calls and offer palliative care. But most family physicians won't make these changes until we change the payment system.

An Ontario experiment in group practice that began in the 1980s, the so-called health service organizations (HSOs), failed primarily because some doctors were making too much money, which created political problems for the government of the day, not because they weren't providing excellent, comprehensive care. Many think that a little "tweaking" of the design would have closed the loopholes and made this experiment a success. There are still some HSOs operating in Ontario, but all new doctors who join these practices are paid according to the fee-for-service regime.

Too bad these pioneering group practices are operating within a larger system that remains dysfunctional in a number of important ways and that doesn't encourage or reward their good behaviour. They've learned to talk to their patients, but the other solitudes in the system aren't talking to them—at least not as often and not as effectively as they could and should be. They are expert clinicians who follow evidence-based practice, who take the time to listen to their patients. I know a story of an obstetrician who complained that he could tell the patients from the CLSCs because they asked too many questions! These clinics provide health care that places the needs of the patient over the convenience of the doctor. They are part of the solution.

Future docs

In a recent speech to a graduating medical school class, Monique Bégin summed up how our system has to change to create the kind of doctors we're going to need in the twenty-first century: (1) Medical education must change to become more responsive to patients' needs; (2) We must forge links between the various sectors and solitudes of the health care world, between traditional medicine (sickness care), health promotion, and disease prevention (public health policy), and the social and environmental determinants of health (poverty, violence, environment).

A few years ago, when I was a member of the board of the Ontario Medical Association, a group of interns and residents were picketing outside OMA headquarters. These young hospital doctors were upset at the proposed restricting of their OHIP billing numbers, the latest in a long line of patchwork attempts at cost containment and at fixing physician maldistribution. The then chief executive of the OMA asked me to go down and talk to them—maybe he thought they'd listen to a woman. When I talked to these young physicians, men and women both, I suggested that perhaps they were preoccupied with fighting old battles that weren't getting us anywhere. I asked them to join me in building a new medical future. I promised that I would be right there beside them, fighting for their right to practise in a system that rewards good medicine, not high-volume medicine, making sure that they were well paid to provide the very best care possible. But they weren't listening. I hope some of them are now.

We doctors need to get down off our pedestals, take off our white lab coats, and share the power. (Have you ever wondered why on earth your family doctor needs to wear a lab coat in order to "talk" to you?) Specialists and family physicians alike must not only listen to their patients, but learn from them and learn to respect what they know. As Sir William Osler taught, "It is more important to know the patient with the disease than the disease within the patient."

Many doctors are already becoming part of the solution. Their numbers are growing. But they can't solve our health care "crisis" on their own.

Part Three

The Patient

5

Don't Blame the Patient

In my family practice, I was lucky. I had great patients. When I hear about the 85 per cent of patients clogging ERs that don't have to be there, I can see how tempting it is to blame patients for many of the problems in our health care system. From the point of view of those on the inside—the overworked providers of health care—patients can seem demanding and difficult and unreasonable. From the point of view of the bureaucrats who measure and monitor the system, it can seem as if patients represent a bottomless well of health care demands, that the more you give them, the more they will want. In reality, however, the patient is seldom the real source of the problem.

Patients as statistics

In the brave new world of downsizing and restructuring, hospitals are under pressure to look at patients in terms of their cost efficiency. These days each hospital is rated on the basis of various criteria aimed at measuring just how well it is doing its job. One of the key criteria is a category called "average length of stay." Under this heading, the statistician records the amount of time each admitted patient spends in the hospital, then adds the numbers together and divides by the total number of patients admitted. The lower the average length of stay, so goes the theory, the better job a hospital is doing because the less public money it is spending per patient admitted.

Consider the case of a person suffering a heart attack who dies before reaching the coronary care unit but minutes after being admitted to the hospital. Shortest length of stay imaginable, right? Yet this "stay" is lumped in with all the others, skewing the figures and making hospitals that keep fewer patients alive longer look better. Sound crazy? Definitely. But it's not the only misleading aspect of the way hospitals look at patients when they look at them as statistics.

In some ways, the worst patient of all, from the hospital's point of view, is a patient who's well enough to ask questions and smart enough to know which questions to ask. In the bad old world of medicine designed for the convenience of physicians and nurses and hospital administrators, the patient who talks back to the nurse or the doctor is a pain in the neck. She makes their jobs more time-consuming. He adds stress to an already stressful workplace.

Such patients are often those who know enough to bring along an advocate. Long before the recent spate of hospital downsizings, I would advise my patients, "Never go to the hospital alone. Always bring someone with you who can advocate on your behalf." With nursing staff now cut to the bone and doctors more overworked than ever, patients should never enter a hospital without someone to stand up for their rights, make sure they don't fall through the cracks, maybe even empty their bed pan. Of course, patients with advocates are the worst sort of patients from the hospital's point of view. They are the ones who complain the most and who demand the best care. They tend to be the most time-consuming patients. Some patients now hire private-duty nurses to act as their advocates. In a reformed system this should no longer be necessary.

This reality means that the best patients are the patients who put up and shut up. Often these patients are people already marginalized in our society. Visit almost any hospital ward these days and you'll know what I'm talking about. The patients who often seem to get lost in the shuffle are the elderly, the immigrants who speak little or no English, the poor who don't feel they have a right to complain. I have seen elderly patients sitting alone in hospital corridors, vainly struggling to catch the eye of the nurses and doctors who rush by.

This situation creates a *de facto* two-tier system of care within our big hospital complexes, a system where the educated, well-informed, and demanding patients get better care than those who don't know what questions to ask or who have no one to ask the questions for them. Recent data suggesting that the better off go to specialists more often is evidence of this trend. Yet from the point of view of hospitals trying to make do with less and to turn over their beds faster so as to reduce their "length of stay" statistics, informed patients, patients who ask questions about their care, are problem patients. Some of these patients are the ones with engaged family doctors who coach them through the hospital experience. A great family physician is a great leveller of the care gap between rich and poor.

We can't blame patients or hospitals for this situation, which is really the result of top-down reforms aimed at the bottom line. Patients are too often seen as problems because that's how the provincial health bureaucracies see them.

Too many patients

The biggest problem that patients cause is that there are simply too many of them for the system. Right now the Canadian population is still relatively young and not as demanding of the health care system as it will be in a few years. But as I pointed out in chapter 2, the baby boom generation, the postwar population bulge, is heading for its senior years at a time when life expectancy is increasing, which means more and more older people needing more and more medical care. According to some predictions, this baby boom bulge will put increasing stress on Canadian medicare in the next decade, a stress that will peak around the year 2020. Here's how David Foot explains what will happen in *Boom, Bust & Echo 2000*: "By the second decade of the new century, when the front edge of the boom enters its senior years, our health care system will be confronted with sharply increased demand. How much will demand for health care services increase? Reliance on doctors turns upward in a person's 40s and continues to increase gradually. Those in their late 70s need doctors twice as often as their lifetime average and those in their later 80s need them 2½ times as often. Reliance on hospitals increases sharply in the mid-50s. By their late 70s, people use hospitals five times more than lifetime average rate of use. Those who survive until their late 80s use hospitals 12 times more than their lifetime average."

The wave of aging boomers is a real problem, but I like the evidence that we're not just getting older, we're getting healthier. *Toronto Star* columnist Richard Gwyn hit the nail squarely when he wrote, "True, we're all getting wrinklier. But we're also incomparably healthier than we've ever been—

better food, more exercise, less drinking, less smoking." As Gwyn also points out, "The principal cause of health-care cost increases is neither demography or technology. It's because we've become a nation of pill-pushers." And much of this pill-pushing stems from lack of patient education.

Blossom Wigdor, the former chief psychologist at St. Mary's Veterans Hospital in Montreal, notes that the fastest-growing segment of the population is over eighty-five and that 12 per cent of Canadians are now over sixty-five. Yet older Canadians don't necessarily place a higher burden on the system. Longer life expectancy does not inevitably mean that individuals spend more years in poor health. Compared with twenty years ago, older adults can expect improved quality and extended length of life. Aging does not necessarily result in a continuous decline in health. Close to half of the seniors who reported fair or poor health in 1994/95 reported an improvement in 1998/99. In fact, Statistics Canada's recent survey *How Healthy Are Canadians?* confirms that the extra years we've gained with increases in life expectancy are healthy years. Regardless of age, the majority of the most expensive health care—especially care involving hospital stays—happens in the last twelve months of a person's life no matter how old he or she is at the time of death. The rest of the time, much of the cost of looking after older people stems from overdosage of drugs which they may or may not need or non-compliance with appropriate prescriptions.

Yes, the combination of our growing population and the aging baby boom will put greater demands on our health care system. But if we reform the system wisely, these demands will be met more and more in non-hospital—i.e., less expensive—settings. There will be more people to treat, it's true, but the system will be better at keeping them healthy and will less often provide them with treatments they don't need or don't want.

Also contributing to our healthier and longer lives will be an increasing sense of individual responsibility for individual health. As the *World Health Report* 2000 eloquently articulated, "The person who seeks health care is of course a consumer—as with other products and services—and may also be a co-producer of his or her health, in following good habits of diet, health, hygiene and exercise, and complying with medication or other recommendations of providers. But he or she is also the physical object to which all such care is directed." Thus the patient must take some of the responsibility for some of the care that he or she may eventually require. The WHO report quoted British neurologist and Renaissance man Jonathan Miller: "Of all the objects in the world, the human body has a peculiar status: it is not only possessed by the person who has it, it also possesses and constitutes him. Our body is quite different than all the other things we claim as our own. We can lose money, books and even houses and still remain recognizably ourselves, but it is hard to give any intelligible sense to the idea of a disembodied person. Although we speak of our bodies as premises that we live in, it is a special form of tenancy: our body is where we can always be contacted."

Some of us take better care of our bodies than others, but, as the report went on to explain, this asset called health is subject to large and unpredictable risks that are mostly independent of one another. Nonetheless, as consumers and "co-producers" the ultimate sustainability of our health care systems will depend on each of us looking after ourselves better.

There are hopeful trends and worrisome ones. *How Healthy Are Canadians?* 2000 found that the proportion of twenty- to twenty-four-year-olds who are at least moderately physically active in their leisure time increased between 1994/95 and 1998/99. But it also noted that the prevalence of smoking among teenagers has increased. And over the past five years, 45 per cent of Canadian males between the ages of twenty and twenty-four indulged in binge drinking (at least five drinks on one occasion) at least once a month.

One of the few things I disliked about being a family doctor was having to go through the motions of telling patients what they already knew: stop smoking; you need to lose some weight so your knee doesn't hurt so much; no more than twelve portions of alcohol per week; get more exercise. Finding the teachable moment was the key, the moment when their bodies started talking back loudly enough that they were prepared to listen. Screenwriter John Hunter calls this body betrayal!

Poor patients are a problem

Far more costly than looking after aging middle-class boomers like me is health care for the growing number of poor people in our society. The latest statistics show that 18 per cent, or more than 5.3 million Canadians, live below the poverty line. As study after study has shown, poorer people are less healthy and, on average, use the health care system more. We should be particularly concerned about the children who live in poverty. Statistics Canada's 1991 report on the health status of children found that "in our poorest neighbourhoods infant mortality is still two-thirds higher than those in our richest neighbourhoods." It also found that "the children of parents with a low level of education are more likely to have poorer perceived health and are less likely to enjoy unbroken good health."

The Patient

Dr. Fraser Mustard, founder of the Canadian Institute of Advanced Research, has proven that a sub-optimal early childhood experience not only harms the child's future potential but also increases the incidence of chronic diseases. The awareness of the need for aggressive support for those early years is gaining attention, from the Vancouver Board of Trade to the Rotary Club of Toronto. We can't afford not to. When it comes to all children, positive interventions, particularly in the early years, can make a huge difference. The late Dr. Paul Steinhauer was a child advocate who developed the "Well Street Index," a measure of the well-being of Canada's children and youth, to emphasize that measuring child development is as important to our society as the Wall Street Index is to the economy.

I'm not among those who believe that poverty is a self-inflicted condition that can be cured by an injection of moral fibre or a strong dose of workfare. Poverty is a symptom of deeper social ills that the health care system can't treat on its own. These ills can be grouped together under what policy thinkers refer to as "the social determinants of health." No reform of the health care system can afford to ignore the underlying factors that determine the health of certain segments of the population.

The long-term answer to health care demand caused by poverty isn't to build more hospitals in poor neighbourhoods and pay doctors more money to practise in poor areas. The long-term answer involves reducing poverty, especially child poverty. Robert Putnam, author of *Bowling Alone*, argues that one of the soundest investments we can make is in "social capital." Putnam defines social capital as the "social networks and the associated norms of reciprocity." Jane Jacobs simply calls it "neighbourliness." But however we define it, Professor Putnam is clear that the opposite—namely, social isolation—is as negative for health status as chronic smoking.

Looked at in this manner, many social welfare expenditures are health care expenditures, at least in part. Aren't free school breakfasts a health care expense? What about elder day care and social clubs for seniors? What about methadone programs for addicted drug users? Or counselling for single mothers?

Recently, Dr. Gina Brown of McMaster University conducted a most revealing study, *When the Bough Breaks*, of single mothers on welfare. When these mothers were given various supports—day care, employment advice, family counselling, a recreational program for their older kids—their health care needs dropped sharply. With just one of these programs in place, 10 per cent were off welfare in one year; with all of them, 20 per cent dropped off the welfare rolls.

I vividly remember the day a few years ago when former Health minister Monique Bégin asked current Health minister Allan Rock the following question, "How on earth do you do your job now that Health is separate from Welfare?" Bégin was referring to the fact that the two areas used to be lumped under one department called Health and Welfare. They were split apart by the federal Tories at the end of their reign. Whether or not the two are under one department, welfare and wellness are inseparable.

Women are problem patients

Women consume more health care than men. According to Heather MacLean of the Centre for Research in Women's Health, they account for 61 per cent of all doctor visits, 59 per cent of prescription drug purchases, and 67 per cent of all hospital procedures. Does this mean they overuse the system? Definitely not. It is true that a woman's physiology makes her more likely to use the services of a physician. For instance, women get pregnant, which means prenatal visits to a physician. Sound practices require care during pregnancy even for otherwise healthy women. Childbirth sometimes has complications; breast-feeding often requires support. Nor is every pregnancy or every delivery problem-free. Over her lifetime, a woman's reproductive organs must be continually checked and can be the site of many problems, from an ovarian cyst to infertility, menstrual problems, and breast cancer. In this narrowly defined sense, women as a group need more health care than men.

As I learned in my own practice, women also seem to be more willing than men to ask questions, and not just about their own health. Women use the system more than men because they tend to assume responsibility for the health care of their entire families. This is most evident in family practice. When a woman says she's got a great family doctor, one of the things she means is that she can talk to her doctor about anything, including the health of her immediate and even extended family. These kinds of conversations take time. If a doctor is churning through as many patients as possible every day, these are conversations to be avoided. Some doctors even have a rule that each patient can discuss only one complaint per visit!

Let's not blame women for overusing the system. Instead, let's educate all patients, both men and women, so that they'll know how to ask the right questions and take on even greater responsibility for their own health care and the health of their extended families.

The patient as overconsumer

Yes, some patients do abuse the system by overusing it or using it inappropriately. When family doctors get together to gossip and complain—as all professional groups do from time to time—they love to talk about these sorts of patients. For example, one day a Bay Street lawyer who'd wrecked his knee while skiing came to see one of my partners at Bedford Medical. He wanted help in applying for Wheel-Trans, the public transportation provided for people with disabilities. What my colleague told this well-heeled gentleman with a well-developed sense of personal entitlement was: "Call a taxi."

Yes, some patients practise doctor shopping in an excessive way. Some bounce from doctor to doctor like a pinball in a pinball machine. I was once the eighth doctor to see a woman who was looking for an obstetrician. She'd been to see seven other physicians before she landed in my office. Clearly her original family physician, who didn't feel competent enough in obstetrics, had done a very poor job of referring her in the first place or this would never have happened.

Some patients even keep separate doctors for separate purposes. I have one acquaintance who always has two family physicians. One he goes to when he needs a proper consultation. This one will give him all the time he needs when he has something complicated to discuss. The other he goes to when he thinks he's got an urgent problem. That one will see him right away and write him a prescription.

And what about the patients who insist on unnecessary drugs—an antibiotic for their cold—or unnecessary tests or unnecessary procedures—even unnecessary operations? These people do exist, but in my experience they are few and they generally respond well to explanation instead of medication. What they need more than medicine is their doctor's time.

The myth that great numbers of people overuse the system prevails, yet the best estimates suggest their number is miniscule—probably no more than 1 per cent of the patient population truly abuse the system. My patients rarely demanded an unnecessary test or treatment once I'd taken the time to explain why it wasn't needed—obstetrical ultrasounds were the exception.

Reforms that would make the health care system more transparent, that would provide patients with much more information about what constitutes quality care, and about what sort of questions they should be asking their doctors will save the system money in the long run. Opponents of such reforms argue that they will create more demanding patients who will put the system under even greater stress. My own experience of general practice, where I learned and benefited from informed patients, makes me an advocate of these reforms.

Study after study backs me up: keeping patients in the dark, not knowing what questions to ask, doesn't work. The more teens get sex education, the lower the teen pregnancy rate. The more a patient knows the "why" and "how" of a proposed therapy, the greater the "buy-in" and the better the compliance with that therapy. The informed patient is more likely to get the right treatment, follow it properly, and then get well. Patients are frequently very good at administering their own health care programs, once they've been set on the right course. Studies have shown that when patients are responsible for controlling their own pain medication—in the days following surgery or in the face of chronic disease—they medicate themselves less than the normally prescribed levels dictated by common practice.

To me, a well-informed but demanding patient is a better patient. This doesn't mean that patients never make unreasonable requests. It's the job of a doctor to help the patient see what's reasonable and what isn't.

I remember many shifts at Sick Kids where the child presented with vomiting and diarrhoea. The treatment of choice was clear fluids—flat ginger ale, chicken soup—and then a diet of bananas, rice, applesauce, and toast. But parents were often very reluctant to leave without a prescription. I must confess even I was delighted when a new product was invented as an excellent clear-fluid replacement treatment for gastroenteritis. It meant I could actually write something down on a piece of paper that the parents could go and buy at the pharmacy. It made us all feel better!

Prescribing to placate the patient happens all the time under our fee-for-service payment model. It takes much longer to explain to patients that a condition doesn't need a prescription than to write one out. If you are paid a set fee for each service, you have a strong incentive to spend less time per patient so that you see more patients. The more pieces you can get through in an hour, the higher your income in the fee-for-service system. If you look at patients as piecework, a well-informed patient who asks questions is your worst nightmare.

The "worst" patients in the world of medical piecework are those who require lots of time but generate relatively few billable medical interventions. At the top of this list are people in the process of dying, whose primary need is for palliative care. Thank goodness there still seem to be lots of doctors who will essentially "volunteer" their time to work with the terminally ill—as the AIDS epidemic has demonstrated. Near the top of the not-wanted list are the elderly. We must now rely on the dedication of doctors willing to take on the increasingly important and relatively poorly paid specialties of geriatrics and palliative care.

Dr. Willy Molloy, the author and geriatrician from Hamilton, Ontario, proved that the elderly patients shipped to hospital from nursing homes, who then get "the works," cost the system huge amounts of money and live less long than the patients who completed his dying with dignity questionnaire, "Let Me Decide," and refused hospital interventions! Sometimes the patients don't even demand the extra care, it's just a systemic knee-jerk response that is unkind and unsafe.

Don't blame the patient or the doctor

Let's not blame the patients or the doctors for our health care problems. Our problems stem from a system that encourages hospitals and health bureaucrats and solo doctors to look at patients in a negative way, a system that makes it harder for the various health care solitudes to work together. I'd like to see a shift in the fundamental philosophy of Canadian medicare to one that promotes the most educated, best-informed, and most demanding patients possible, patients who take more, not less, responsibility for their bodies and keeping them healthy. We need a system where the patient isn't part of the problem but part of the solution.

6

The Patient
Is Part of the Solution

The informed patient

In my twenty-five years of medical practice, only once did a patient whose baby I had delivered come in for her six-week post-partum check-up unsure why she'd had a Caesarean section. When she expressed her concern, I remember being very upset. I was upset that I had failed her. I'd always considered it part of my job to keep my patients informed every step of the way. A patient who didn't know the reason for a particular treatment was a patient I had let down.

Few family doctors have had anything like my good fortune in treating a group of patients that included so many knowledgeable people. But not all my patients were as knowledgeable as those extraordinary women who came into my office with copies of *Our Bodies, Our Selves* tucked under their arms. Informed patients don't grow on trees. They have to be cultivated, nurtured. Doctors and nurses must do much of the nurturing. We should all be cultivating more informed patients, patients who know good care from bad care, patients who keep us on our toes.

If you are one of these patients, you will sometimes leave your doctor's office with your question unanswered, usually because the doctor has admitted that he or she doesn't know the answer to the question but has promised that together "we will find out." However, the empowered patient will never leave the office without having asked the question!

When I hosted the television phone-in show "Doctor on Call," I was astounded how often callers hadn't been given the information they needed to understand their diagnosis or treatment. Sometimes a diagnosis becomes apparent only over time. But throughout that time the patient and the doctor must work together to identify the clues that will solve the puzzle. My favourite on-air interactions involved coaching a caller to go back to his or her own doctor with a better question. If the patient is prepared, the doctor will soon learn what it means to be part of a more equitable physician–patient relationship!

Retraining your doctor

I used to feel uncomfortable when a patient asked me a question to which I could only answer "I don't know, but I'll find out." Later I understood that the finding out was an important part of my education as a family physician. It meant consulting colleagues, searching the medical literature, sometimes talking to alternative-care practitioners such as midwives and chiropractors. Sometimes it meant waiting for the "tincture of time" to sort out the problem.

Informed, questioning patients make their doctors into better clinicians. My definition of a poor doctor is one who never has to say "I don't know." Part of my definition of a good doctor is someone who knows the limits of his or her knowledge. Finding out the answers to these questions was a crucial part of my training. I wouldn't have become as good a doctor without the questions my patients asked me. The body is very humbling and mysterious. Patients do know when their bodies are talking back. There is nothing more devastating to a patient with pain than to be told that the x-ray is normal, and therefore there is nothing wrong. The patient with pain knows that something is wrong and deserves to be told what has been ruled out and what will be done to get to the cause of the pain.

Patients can retrain physicians, but first they have to overcome their perception that doctors have all the power. Many people who wouldn't hesitate to tell a waiter in a restaurant that they were unhappy with the service wouldn't dream of saying the same thing to their doctors. Some are able to tell off the doctor's staff but become buttery sweet as soon as they enter the consulting room. Physician education requires that the patient give feedback directly.

Changing doctors' attitudes will take time, but the process is already under way. One of the leaders in physician retraining is Pat Kelly, a fearless advocate for those with breast cancer who now heads an organization called PISCES (Partnering in Self-help Community Education and Support). One of PISCES's programs teaches cancer patients how to get what they need from their physicians "with a sense of humour" so that the physician won't feel criticized or put down. As Sarah Scott reported in the January 1999 issue of *Chatelaine*, "These new medical consumers want to be equal partners, sharing decisions rather than just following doctors' orders. They're colliding with doctors who practise old-style medicine."

Given that advocates for cancer patients have been trailblazers in improving doctor–patient communication, it's not surprising that two promising pilot programs under the heading "It Helps to Talk" have recently been initiated by the Manitoba Cancer Treatment and Research Foundation. (They are jointly sponsored by Health Canada and the provincial cancer societies of both Manitoba and Nova Scotia.) The programs provide both patients and doctors with communication tips and tools. Their goal is to help patients to better articulate their concerns and to better prepare for each appointment with their doctors.

The responsible patient

The patients who educated me, and who continue to educate other doctors, have knowledge and self-possession. They also have a sense of responsibility: they are prepared to take charge of their own health care, become informed, and be active on their own behalf. One cannot, of course, force patients to behave responsibly. Voluntary assumption of responsibility produces much better results. Responsible patients are by no means the cure-all. Even the most conscientious patient cannot force the family physician's office to provide an around-the-clock on-call system.

One of the advantages of reorganizing primary care would be a commitment to a twenty-four-hour-a-day, seven-days-a-week on-call system. Soon, practices not providing this comprehensive care will have a much tougher time getting patients. I somehow don't think that patients will prefer to spend four hours in an emergency department for something that could have been handled over the phone by a family doctor with access to his or her record and the ability to provide appropriate follow-up.

Responsible patients are also aware of how much the inappropriate use of emergency departments costs the system both in money and in the time of highly trained emergentologists and emergency room nurses. It's not surprising that patients dropping into the local ER on a Sunday afternoon with a two-month history of fatigue don't feel particularly welcome. We can and must retrain these patients too.

Communication between patient and physician is a two-way street. In medical school, we were taught that 90 per cent of almost any diagnosis derives from the patient's history. Hence the importance of doctors becoming expert listeners. But the patient also has to be willing to talk. During my last year of medical school, I spent two months doing an elective in obstetrics in Barbados. Taking a history from many of my Barbadian patients was like pulling teeth. Rather than give me specific symptoms, they would say only that they had "the bad feels." I soon learned that "the bad feels" could mean anything from tuberculosis to a tubal pregnancy! When I asked more questions, they inevitably replied, "You're the doctor!" These patients had been so indoctrinated with the notion that the doctor was some sort of god that they seemed to believe I didn't need any help from them.

For patients, taking responsibility for their part in the doctor-patient relationship means providing complete information to the doctor as well as asking questions and insisting on answers. It means keeping track of their own medications and being up to date on medical and family history. It means questioning treatments that aren't backed up by clinical evidence, as so many of my early patients did.

Before you visit any doctor, write down a list of questions so that you don't forget to ask them. Here is a checklist to go over before every visit to a physician. Make a copy and take it with you. (For a checklist on how to go about choosing a family physician in the first place, see Appendix A.)

The Patient

What to bring to every appointment

1. Your health card.
2. All the medications you are currently taking—especially if they were prescribed by someone else!
3. Any updates or changes to your family history.
4. Results of any recent tests for a chronic condition, including high blood pressure test results.
5. Information about any allergies that might affect your treatment (for example, drugs, latex, lactose).
6. Your timetable or work schedule so that you can book follow-up appointments, if needed.

Questions to ask your doctor

About Tests

1. Do I really need this test? What can you do for me without this test? Is it just routine?
2. Where do I go to get it and what are the hours? Do I need an appointment?
3. How should I prepare for the test? (Do I need to fast, bring a urine sample?)
4. How will you communicate the results? (No news is good news? You'll call me either way? I have to call you?)
5. How accurate/reliable is it? (Frequency of false positives/negatives, etc.)
6. How long will the test take and is there anything I shouldn't be doing afterwards? (Driving? Drinking? Exercise?)

About Prescriptions

1. Do I need this prescription? Are you sure I need an antibiotic for this? (Learn the difference between a virus—a cold,

the flu—and a bacterial infection. Antibiotics work on bacterial infections, not viruses.)

2. What are the side effects?

3. If I'm allergic to X, will I be able to take what you're prescribing?

4. Can I take this if I am also taking Y?

5. Is it expensive? Is there a less expensive generic version that's just as good?

6. Will I have to have my blood tested or any other tests while I'm on this drug?

7. Are there repeats on this? How do I get the prescription renewed if I need to? Can I do this by phone?

8. Is there anything I can't do while taking this drug? (Drive? Drink alcohol? Take strenuous exercise?)

9. Do I have to take the whole prescription or can I stop when I feel better?

About Surgery

1. Do I really need this surgery? Are there any alternatives?

2. Where will it be done and who will do it? What's the success rate for this procedure? What are the risks? What are the risks if I don't have the surgery?

3. Why is this doctor the right one to perform this surgery? Can you tell me about this person's background and qualifications and about the institution where the operation will take place?

4. Will I be able to meet the surgeon before the procedure? Where? When? How?

5. Will I need a general anesthetic and how will the anesthetist be chosen? How do I communicate with this doctor about my health/allergies?

6. Does this hospital have an intake procedure or a pre-op procedure and how can I get into it?

7. Will you be involved? How do I reach you?
8. What happens after my surgery?

If you are calling for telephone advice, make sure you're prepared before you pick up the phone. If you're feeling feverish, take your temperature. If you want a prescription to be renewed, make sure you have the telephone number for your pharmacy ready. If you are waiting for the doctor to call you back, stay off the line. Busy signals don't make for good telephone advice.

If a close friend or family member is in hospital, find out what time the doctors make their rounds so that you can be there to ask questions on your relative's or your friend's behalf. Don't go playing telephone tag with the surgeon for two days when you could have cornered him or her right away. Make sure you understand the diagnosis and the prognosis. And make sure you start talking about discharge plans the day your relative or friend enters the hospital. For example, an elderly relative may not be able to return home after a serious illness. Where will this person go after release?

Don't be afraid to ask for a second opinion, but if the second opinion agrees with the first, don't ask for a third. A responsible patient chooses one family physician and stays with him or her, building a relationship based on respect, honesty, and trust. The famous U.S. judge Oliver Wendell Holmes put it this way: "What I call a good patient is one who, having found a good physician, sticks to him for life."

Dr. Irwin Bean, the chief of family medicine at the Wellesley Hospital when I was training there, used to divide patients into three categories: "the sick, the well, and the worried well." For some patients, no amount of education will cure their chronic worry. These patients often take more of a physician's time—because they are sure something is wrong. The patient's body may, for example, be talking back to the sheer stresses of daily life. Fatigue is one of the most common complaints family physicians hear, especially from women who juggle both professional and domestic roles. After many tests, the results may tell it all: "mere mortal, not bionic." The great majority of patients respond well to information that is communicated in a helpful way. As a general rule, patients want to know more. Once they know what you know, they will accept the simplest prescription, even if it is simply reassurance or advice to recharge the battery.

When they know more, they feel better about their care and become better patients. As their knowledge increases, their anxiety decreases. With a trusting doctor–patient relationship, they are more likely to follow the prescribed treatment (and get well) than to look for alternatives—the wasteful process called "doctor shopping."

Good physicians and good patients make for good partnerships. As I argued in chapter 4, "The Doctor Is Part of the Solution," doctors need to start looking at their patients as partners in the health care process. Likewise, the patient must approach the relationship as a partner, not a second-class citizen. Only when the patient feels on an equal footing with his or her physician will he or she have a sense of control. Patients as partners are patients with real power over the kind and quality of their health care. Real partners don't "go elsewhere" without a proper conversation about why.

Patients and best practices

An informed patient who can enter into a genuine partnership with a doctor or other health care provider experiences a greater sense of power within the doctor–patient, professional–non-professional relationship. He or she is more able to see the doctor as an equal, not as an authority figure. Patients who feel more power are going to set higher standards of care. Some of them will join together into self-help or patient-advocacy groups that act as watchdogs of the system in the same way that consumer groups keep an eye on many other industries.

The best quality-control mechanism for our health care system right now is the informed patient. Some, in fact, argue that it's the only quality-control mechanism! If you're not satisfied with your care, discuss it with your doctor before looking for another doctor. If you're not satisfied with the way you were treated during your recent stay in hospital or the way you were bounced from specialist to specialist without ever really getting an answer, tell your family physician. Call the hospital ombudsman.

I realize that some doctors simply won't respond to even the most informed and the best prepared patient. These doctors will have to learn to change their ways. In the short run, no single patient, no matter how well informed, can reform a doctor addicted to bad practices. Accountability mechanisms will need to be built into the system, a subject I tackle in detail in chapter 9.

Medicine should not have less quality control than exists in most industries. And we shouldn't have to wait for the retirements or deaths of those who resist change before change can occur. To paraphrase visionary thinker Jane Jacobs, we cannot afford to wait for progress that only comes funeral by funeral. Patients can accelerate the progress by working on their physicians. I've known some old-fashioned obstetricians who have retired rather than deal with the new breed of more demanding patient. Maybe progress can be made retirement after retirement.

The automotive industry works at ensuring quality through a system of Continuous Quality Improvement (CQI). I'd like to see Canadian patients become part of a CQI mechanism for health care. In order for this to happen, patients must have access to information on what are known as best practices.

Best practices are the most successful treatments available. They are the best practices based on the latest clinical evidence, the best evidence-based medicine. Canadian patients should have access to an annually updated guide-book to best practices. Where patients already have such guidelines, they have worked wonders. The excellent new Canadian Health Network (see Appendix B), with its 500 partner organizations, is now focused on information for disease prevention and health promotion. But in its next phase, with the help of Dr. Alan Bernstein and the fabulous new Canadian Institute of Health Research, it could provide an amazing one-stop shopping mall for "best practices."

There is already a great deal of information on best prac-tices available, but it is scattered and not universally acces-sible. Patients can find some of it by joining a patients' self-help group or surfing the Web. The best-informed patients will often be ahead of their doctors. I vividly remember the first time a breast cancer patient asked if she should be having her surgery at a particular time in her menstrual cycle after she'd read a study that suggested there were good times and bad times for surgery. I had many AIDS patients who told me about new drug therapies before I read about them. (AIDS patients were often ahead of their doctors because treatments were changing so fast.)

But much of the information out there, particularly on the Web, is questionable or even laughable. One morning, when I was still hosting "Doctor on Call," a researcher brought me a downloaded article on cholesterol that was a thinly disguised propaganda piece from a cattle breeders' association. (The article even spelled the word *cholesterol* incorrectly!) Television medical dramas can also inform patients in the wrong way. I remember the day after a certain episode of the long-running ER when every patient in my pre-natal clinic had serious concerns about dying from a Caesarean section.

In such cases, it is up to the doctor to help the patient separate the good information from the bad and the imagined illness from the legitimate concern. But it's clear from the Canadian Health Network that an easily accessible source of reliable health information is a tremendous resource for patients.

Informed choice

The catchphrase that encapsulates the patient as part of the solution is *informed choice*. For patients to make wise choices they must be given the appropriate information and they must be welcomed as partners in the decision-making process. A health care decision is taken jointly by the patient and the physician, but in the final analysis it must be the patient's decision.

Informed choice implies a delicate balance between the patient's right to decide and the doctor's responsibility to treat. It occurs when doctors become good teachers and good listeners who create safe environments in which their patients can ask and learn and then decide.

Informed choice gives power to the patient, which is where it belongs. When a patient makes an informed choice, he or she becomes part of the solution and is ready to play the pivotal role on the new health care team.

Part Four

The Plan

7

Playing on
the New Health Care Team

The road to reform

It was not long ago that the late Dr. Adam Linton, past president of the Ontario Medical Association, accused the medical profession of suffering from "mural dyslexia: they can't read the writing on the wall." Dr. Linton would undoubtedly be encouraged by the increasing number of progressive thinkers in his profession, but reforming Canada's troubled health care system won't happen overnight. There will be a period of transition and more than a few bumps on the road to redemption. There will be a lot of kicking and screaming from certain interest groups who see reform as a threat to their incomes and their comfortable positions, and from politicians who sometimes confuse short-term gains and long-term solutions and are therefore afraid to tackle the tough issues. But we are already closer to a system that really works than you might think. There are beacons of reform from coast to coast, places where promising new models are being tried and old wisdoms built upon. More and more *medical professionals* and *health care administrators* are coming out of their ivory towers and looking favourably on new alternatives.

In my talks these days, I often compare health care reform to a Zamboni. I ask my audiences: "Who will drive it? Who will be under the tire treads?" The drivers will be those who believe in a patient-centred system, fully integrated, with accountability built in at every level, and strong incentives for the best of best practices. It will be a system where disease prevention and health promotion are as important or more important than sickness care. The drivers on the road to reform will be those who are willing to experiment with the alternatives until we find just the right mix for the twenty-first century.

Many of these alternatives—the details of how we will reform and restructure our health care system—are still being developed and refined. But the clear outlines of the new system and a remarkable amount of the fine print are already in place. Those of us who believe that Canada's publicly funded, universally accessible health care system can and must be saved—and that it can be made far better for everyone in the process—share a vision of what the reformed, user-friendly system will look like and how the public will experience it. In this new world, the various providers of sickness care and health care will be part of an integrated whole instead of a collection of solitudes that seldom talk to each other and far too seldom work together for the best interests of the patient. Future health care in Canada will have everyone playing on the same team.

What's so great about a team?

Top-down, highly centralized organizational structures are not the way of the future. Increasingly, complex organizations and systems are organized horizontally rather than hierarchically and are broken down into teams. On a good team, two plus two equals five; a team is greater than the sum of its parts. Teamwork is generally acknowledged as the modern way to manage. It gives individuals more sense of purpose and it produces better results.

Getting the best out of each member of the team means including every member in the decision-making process, which is predicated on a relationship between team members where each respects the knowledge and expertise of the other. Distinguished professor and social activist Ursula Franklin tells a story that perfectly illustrates the value of inclusive decision making.

Franklin recalls being invited to a public school to facilitate a professional development day on children at risk. She agreed to attend as long as all the staff were invited, not just the principal, the guidance counsellor, and the teachers. After raising several objections, the principal reluctantly agreed. At the very first session, one of the janitors raised his hand. When he spoke, he told his colleagues how he always knew the children from the violent homes: they were there waiting when he opened the school at 7:00 a.m. In the next session, a woman working in the school kitchen rhymed off the children who weren't getting enough to eat at home and so came to school hungry: they were the ones who offered to help clear the plates at lunch so they could eat the leftovers. By the end of the day, the principal and the teachers were amazed at how simple the task of identifying those at risk had become. You just had to include everyone in the discussion.

Over the years of my association with Women's College Hospital, I've seen how well this type of decision making works in a health care setting. At WCH, we have always involved all the affected staff in any task force. Time and again, insight and innovation have come from an unexpected person: for example, the obstetrics ward clerk who really understood the difficulty of trying to enforce the rules around inducing labour to petulant obstetricians who thought the rules were for everyone's benefit except his (or hers), or the increasing sick calls by nurses asked to work short-staffed when others were off sick.

WCH's neonatal intensive care unit allowed each member of the team to participate at his or her optimal level—a pharmacist, a respiratory technician, or a nurse could all change an order that had been previously written by a doctor for a patient. By the time the doctor co-signed the change, the decision had often already been carried out. At WCH, nurses chaired committees and ran units such as the sexual assault–care centre. Nurse examiners were trained for that unit, then they ran courses to train trainers for other units.

I've seen how teams deliver better health care both at Women's College and in my own group practice. I've seen how teamwork can put the patient at the centre where he or she belongs.

Where does the reform start?

As far as I'm concerned, the answer to this question is not rocket science. We start where most of us first deal with the health care system and where most of us spend most of our health care time: with the family doctor. We start with primary care because even before the recent round of hospital cuts, closures, and amalgamations, health care was moving from its traditional focus on hospitals towards more health care in community settings. We start with the family doctor because he or she is the health care provider closest to the patient and best able to give the patient real power and discretion.

Starting with the family doctor makes sense for all sorts of reasons. Family doctors are specialists at treating the whole person as part of a family and a community, not just as a medical complaint or question. That's why family doctors are in an ideal position to judge whether a complaint is primarily medical or social or psychological. They know the patient as a human being, not simply as a list of presenting symptoms.

We already have the resources to put family doctors at the centre of future health care. Canadian medical schools turn out family doctors who can practise anywhere. (No wonder so many newly graduated "platinum trained" family physicians are being lured south of the border, where family physicians are in dangerously short supply. They are the best case managers that American health management organizations can hire because they have highly developed skills in communicating with patients and know how to deliver more cost-effective care.) More important, the vast majority of Canadians, over 90 per cent, already have a doctor they regard as their primary physician. If we put the family doctor at the hub, we won't have to reinvent the wheel.

The family physician is the patient's health care advocate and guide. He or she is supposed to know the system and how to navigate it for best results, and know how to help each patient get the most appropriate care and the best care. The family doctor is as interested in keeping you healthy as in treating your sickness. The family doctor is your health care champion.

Finally, the family doctor provides the best care at the least cost. As I pointed out in Part One, we waste money each time a patient ends up in the wrong part of the system at the wrong time. The cost comes in terms of too many drugs prescribed and, often, in the negative side effects of too many drugs and drugs improperly prescribed. We also waste money whenever a high-priced specialist treats a non-specialized complaint, for example, when an ear, nose and throat specialist treats someone with the common cold. Things get even more wasteful when a specialist refers a patient to another specialist who refers the patient to another specialist, and so on. The patient as bouncing ball from specialist to specialist is bad for the patient and is very costly to the system. Patients with a doctor-coach have always been the haves. Patients without these advocates have always been the have-nots.

I have never apologized for the fact that power and influence can affect timely access to care. But I have always believed that it should be the power and influence of a great family physician that allows him or her to advocate for appropriate care whether the patient lives in a homeless shelter or a million-dollar penthouse. Family doctors also have a responsibility to modify expectations in this "instant everything" world. When a two-week wait is totally appropriate, it is the job of the family doctor to provide that reassurance.

The primary-care team

Primary care means the care at the front line provided by family doctors, pharmacists, nurse practitioners, community clinics, nursing homes and home care practitioners, public health nurses, midwives and by some naturopaths and other complementary care practitioners. For most of us, it's the only kind of medical care we need for most of our lives. For many of us, it's the only medicine we'll ever experience. The best way to deliver primary care is through a team of experts working together. The two key players on the primary-care team are the family doctor—the expert about the way the system works—and the patient—the expert about whether his or her body is working normally—but all other players in primary care will be on the same team.

The primary-care team, or group practice of family physicians and other health care professionals, is the model at the centre of Canada's future health care system. As my own experience in the early days of Bedford Medical proved, a group of family physicians working together can provide far better and far more comprehensive care than can the very finest solo practitioner. No single doctor can work twenty-four hours a day, seven days a week, but working together a group of eight to ten doctors can provide round-the-clock care. In our group practice, I got to know the sick patients of all my fellow physicians. And I could consult with the other doctors in the practice in their particular areas of expertise.

Here's the model of group practice that I and many like-minded reformers envision. It's a model where the patient is a full partner who shares responsibility with the physician for his or her own health care.

1. A group practice consists of at least eight family physicians and a mix of other care providers—for example, a nurse, a nurse practitioner, a social worker, a dietician, a psychologist—depending on the needs of its patient population. I'd say that the ideal ceiling for any group practice would be about fifteen doctors. Beyond that number you can't really get to know your colleagues' patients.

2. Every group practice would be "on call" twenty-four hours a day, seven days a week. That means patients would be able to call up their doctor day or night and get a human being qualified to provide medical advice and, if necessary, able to refer them to the appropriate urgent-care facility, whether it's their clinic, emergency room, or all-night dental clinic.

3. Ideally, this group practice will share one office location, enabling the doctors and other professionals to easily and instantly draw on others' expertise. Just as I was able to pop into a colleague's office at Bedford Medical when I needed help, the physicians in a group practice will be better doctors because of the support of their colleagues. Of course, group practices won't spring up over night. There will be resistance from patient-churning city doctors and from those who own and profit from walk-in clinics. In some areas there won't be enough physicians to form a group practice that's physically in one place. Fortunately, the Internet and new information technology now make the "virtual" group practice possible, as a number of pilot projects in several provinces are already demonstrating. Eventually, I would like to see every family physician in Canada part of a primary-care team, whether the group practice is virtual or not, and with access to the patient records for the whole practice population.

4. Each group practice will be responsible for looking after the health of a set number of patients, an approach known as rostering. Patient population numbers will vary considerably depending on demographic make-up and between rural and urban practices, but the average population a single family doctor can excellently serve seems to be about 2,000. Group practices serving a poor population or an inner-city population may have smaller numbers to look after or more budget for nurses, social workers, and so on, to compensate for the complexity of their patient profile. At present, physicians in underserved rural areas have to look after far more patients than their urban counterparts. But as the new system comes into effect, any physician glut in big cities would begin to melt away—the extra doctors won't have any patients—while the group-practice model will

make family practice in areas that are now underserved more attractive.

5. Family physicians in a group practice will no longer be paid a fee for each service they perform. Instead they will be paid according to the total number of patients served by the whole practice. Bonuses built into the payment system could encourage the reaching and exceeding of established health care benchmarks. There could be other financial incentives for doing obstetrics and emergency department shifts, or making house calls. Such bonuses would kick in, for example, when a certain percentage of all the babies in the practice are immunized or when the smoking rate in the practice decreases, and so on. This system will reward doctors for helping their patients stay healthy and happy, rather than for seeing as many as possible per day. Ultimately, I believe that a shift to rostering will mean that the average family doctor will be able to do a better job. Doctors would be better remunerated for keeping more of their patients healthy, as well as for maintaining an audit system for their practice.

6. The payment system can also build in financial incentives for group practices to look after difficult or demanding patient populations, or underserved populations. A bonus system can reward practices that take on tougher or more time-consuming assignments: AIDS patients, for example, or intravenous drug users, or poor people, or elderly patients, or people requiring palliative care, or patients with mental disabilities. Such incentives will have the added advantage of making it more attractive to practise among traditionally underserved patient groups or in underserved areas. (As well as financial incentives, appropriate multidisciplinary teams would be an enormous help.)

7. Advances in information technology will make it possible for every group practice to create a practice profile—a

detailed portrait of its patient population—that is constantly being updated. These practice profiles will enable the group to decide when it needs to hire more staff and what types of skills it needs to add: another nurse practitioner? a geriatric nurse? a social worker? This patient profile will also make it easier to monitor benchmarks. In order, for example, to determine whether a practice is successful in encouraging certain types of preventive testing, it first must know which of its patients would benefit from such tests.

8. Every family doctor will be responsible for continuing his or her medical education, something that's now required only of members of the College of Family Physicians. At present, membership is voluntary, but with the advent of initiatives to audit the ongoing competency of physicians, the College of Family Physicians could be instrumental in helping to design a system that could build upon its Maintenance of Certification program.

9. Each resident of Canada will still have the right to choose his or her family doctor. But the act of choosing will come with very specific responsibilities outlined in a contract between physician and patient that each patient and his or her physician will sign. The contract will commit the patient to consult his or her primary-care physician—or another doctor in that physician's group practice—before consulting any other doctor, whether family physician or specialist. If a patient wishes to change doctors, the existing contract will be terminated at the same time as a new contract is entered into. These primary-care contracts will put an end to fragmented care, which not only costs the system but is often dangerous.

10. Group practices will be accountable for the quality of their care. This kind of ongoing accountability will cut both ways. The group-practice profile will indicate when a group is meeting or exceeding the benchmarks of best practices,

achieving or exceeding an agreed on standard of quality in keeping its population healthy and will be rewarded for this. The individual practitioner will also have his or her own scores.

The patient as captain

If we're all going to play on a primary-care team, we'll need a team captain and a coach. Even the most progressive doctors tend to think of themselves as both coach and captain. (Old habits die hard.) But I beg to differ. If we are really going to adopt a primary-care model where the patient and the doctor are equals who enter into a relationship based on shared responsibility and mutual respect, then the patient—the person who "consumes" medical care and who lives or dies by the result—must be the captain.

The patient as captain is well informed and thus able to ask pointed questions of the physician and expect honest answers that will include all the choices. (In other words, the patient has the right to be wrong.) The patient as captain expects evidence-based practice, not medicine because we've always done it this way before. As captain of the health care team, the patient needs a "playbook" of clinical guidelines, a constantly updated compendium of the most successful treatments available, a guide to the best of "best practices."

Then, if a patient has coronary artery disease or high blood pressure, he or she will know what to expect for treatment. As I've known since my earliest days as a family doctor: better-informed patients don't overuse the system, they use it more wisely and ultimately cost it less. Informed patients aren't more expensive, they are the key to making the new primary-care team work.

The Plan

Many doctors will be a little taken aback the first time they try to prescribe an expensive macrolide antibiotic for a strep throat and the patient looks at the prescription and asks, "Wouldn't just straight penicillin make more sense?" I can't wait until patients have the tools to be part of the solution. With a playbook of clinical guidelines and "best practices" as part of every patient's health care entitlement, we will move towards the sustainable system that we all want.

I can almost hear the objections many readers will raise at this point. How can we expect everyone, regardless of education or social circumstance, to behave in the informed and self-confident way that your highly educated, middle-class patients did? How can you learn to be an informed patient if you're struggling to get by on welfare or wrestling with serious literacy issues or still learning to speak French or English? What if I'm too sick to want to be the captain? Doesn't the patient-centred system you're calling for really mean patient-centred for the well-off and the well-educated and the same old system for the rest of us?

These are good questions, but I think they miss my essential point. Some patients will be better informed than others and will become more skilled at playing the captain's role, just as some consumers become consumer advocates. Diabetes is a disease that crosses all socio-economic lines. Yet thanks to considerable work at patient education, diabetics are increasingly in charge of their own care. They've learned to be captains. If the system assumes that the patient is captain, you'll be surprised how quickly people take to their new role. There's a fair dose of paternalism in the notion that just because people are poorer or didn't go to college they don't have the smarts to ask questions and demand answers. The deeper issue is that the medically disenfranchised in our society don't feel they have the right to ask questions in the first place. Now they will. How will they know they have this right? Because every message they receive about their health care from both federal and provincial governments will remind them. And because it will be part of the job of every family practice to teach them how. In sum, a system designed on the assumption that patients are at the centre—that gives patients respect—will breed more captains.

This having been said, it is true that there will always be some patients who simply can't or won't take on the captain's role. But how will they be worse off than they are in the present system, where they don't think of themselves as having any power at all? These patients may require the additional help of a community health worker, volunteer, family member, or friend. But an enlightened physician/coach who treats them with dignity and then gives them the right to make choices whenever possible is a good start.

The doctor as coach

If the patient is the captain, then the family doctor is the playing coach. As coach, the doctor becomes the patient's advocate and guide through the system, referring him or her to the best specialist, where necessary, discussing the best treatment at length and considering the alternatives, including doing nothing.

The idea of the family doctor as the patient's coach through the system has appealed to me for a long time. For me, the word *coach* acknowledges an important advisory role but implies that the ultimate decision must be made by the player. One of the best compliments I ever got from a patient was that I was a "great coach." This patient, Andrea Esson, was both a lawyer and an amazing coach. She was a level IV instructor for the Canadian Ski Instructors' Alliance and a level III coach for the Canadian Ski Coaches Federation. Andrea was complimenting me on the way I coached her through childbirth, but I began to wonder how much good coaching might apply in other areas of medical practice.

I asked her, "What does good coaching mean? What makes a great coach?" We had many chats about this topic, conversations that ultimately led her to write a paper called "Coaching for Best Performance." In it she concluded that "some health practitioners . . . were natural coaches. Instinctively, they give the information and support necessary to enable the mother to develop appropriate objectives for labour and delivery, and to enhance her performance towards those objectives."

Here's what Andrea says it takes to be a great coach: (1) knowledge; (2) the setting of realistic goals; (3) excellent communication. The sentence "Effective coaching depends on trust" opened the section on knowledge in Andrea's paper. Competitive skiers, women in labour, and patients coming to a family practice need to know that the "coach" is thoroughly knowledgeable about their physiology and about the system in which they are being asked to perform. The coach must be prepared to share information in a way that is understandable and allows for choices that are realistic and flexible.

Realistic goals may simply mean agreeing that you'll never fit into that Size 8 again or just trying to exercise for twenty minutes, three times per week. Sometimes they may mean admitting that you need the nicotine patch or gum for a lot longer than the usual withdrawal period. Once I remember telling a working mother that she should maybe consider buying the new salt- and sugar-free baby food instead of staying up until 1:00 in the morning to Cuisinart her own.

According to Andrea, "Successful coaches are masterful communicators." They must "speak clearly, listen quietly and demonstrate an authentic concern for the well-being of their athletes." Or their patients. Her perception is echoed by the author of "Communication Skills for Coaches," published in 1988 by the Coaching Association of Canada: "Communication is not a matter of techniques or gimmicks, but of sensitivity, understanding and responsiveness toward other people." Not a bad description of a fine family physician.

Many people worry that because family doctors are generalists, they'll miss a serious problem or won't know how to treat one if they do find it. Family doctors as coaches don't know everything. No one doctor does. Family doctors do know when the problem is one they can handle and when their patient should be referred to a specialist or some other part of the system. Knowing when and where to refer is an essential part of the job.

Admitting you are wrong may be the most difficult aspect of coaching for many doctors to accept. We've been conditioned to believe that patients will trust us only if we assume the mantle of high priests. But as medical ethicist Arthur Schafer points out, this almost inevitably has the opposite effect. "If a physician confidently offers a diagnosis or strongly advocates a particular treatment without indicating to the patient that the diagnosis is only tentative or the treatment controversial, then what often results is a drastic undermining of patient confidence and trust. When things go wrong, when the confidently offered diagnosis proves incorrect or the confidently recommended treatment proves inefficacious or even harmful (as often happens), then the physician will have to face patient anger and disillusionment."

The Plan

"Surely," Schafer continues, "it would be preferable if physicians were to assist patients to cope with uncertainties rather than to engage in the pretense that 'doctors know best.' When there are alternative therapies (including the conservative option of doing nothing), surely it is the physician's job to discuss the benefits and burdens of each, and to assist the patient to decide which therapy is best from the patient's point of view." In other words, better to play coach than god—for both the doctor and the patient.

Most family doctors and most patients don't yet think of themselves in these terms. Nurses, by contrast, have long been accustomed to thinking of themselves as members of a team. As André Picard points out in *Critical Care*, nurses are "team players who know their precise role." Picard's definition of a good nurse ought to be the job description for every member of the new health care team: "the ability to listen, to digest information quickly, to analyse, to prioritize, and to act decisively." As family practices come to include more and more nurses and nurse practitioners, you will see more and more nurses as co-coaches, working closely with patients and their family physicians as guides through the system.

One of the family physician's most important jobs in helping patients navigate the system is making referrals. This responsibility acknowledges that, while patients know their bodies best, the coach knows the system best. Knowing when to refer and where to refer is the hallmark of a fine physician. The best coaches often call in outside experts. In our system these physician experts are usually called specialists.

The specialist as consultant

If the doctor is the health care coach on the primary-care team, then the specialist's role resembles that of an assistant coach who is an expert in a particular area of the team's performance: the pitching coach, the batting instructor, the defensive coordinator. Actually, I've never liked the word *specialist*; family doctors are specialists, too; their specialty is looking after the whole person in the context of family and community. But whatever these experts are called, their proper function is as consultants to the controlling partners in the process, the patient and the family doctor.

In health care jargon, specialists deliver what is called "secondary care." That's because they are—or ought to be—the second stage of care a patient experiences. Ordinarily, you are referred to one of these expert consultants by your family doctor. You don't just walk in the door on your own. On the new health care team, the consultant will always report back to the family doctor. It's a question of common sense and good practice. He or she will *never* refer a patient to another specialist without first consulting with the family physician, whose job it is to coordinate the whole team and to guide the patient through the system, to always keep an eye on the big picture. The family doctor will always send a referral note to the specialist or call ahead and the specialist's job isn't done until the consult letter is sent back to the family physician.

Just like family doctors, specialists need to learn to be better listeners. Like family doctors they need to admit when they're wrong or when they just don't know. As Arthur Schafer reminds us, "there is still a great deal of uncertainty and ignorance in medicine." He quotes a former editor of the prestigious *New England Journal of Medicine*, who puts the number of patient visits to doctors that are either "self-limiting (they will get better without treatment) or beyond the capabilities of medicine" at 90 per cent. That's a humbling figure and one all doctors should remember.

The Plan

As specialists adapt to their new role as assistant coaches on the integrated health care team, many of the worst abuses caused by doctor shopping, misdiagnosis, and overmedication will disappear. This subtle but profound shift will save the system untold millions, more likely billions, of dollars. Never again should we see situations where the patient is taking a double dose of medication because the family physician and the specialist have unwittingly both prescribed it.

Hospitals in orbit

When I give speeches calling for health care reform, I often show a picture of the medical system as a solar system, a metaphor that I owe to Roger S. Hunt, president and CEO of the Greater Rochester Health System in New York State. In the bad old days, the hospital was the sun around which all other deliverers of health care orbited like so many lesser planets. The patient was in an orbit somewhere out near Pluto. In the future, with patients and family doctors directing the process, the traditional medical solar system will be turned inside out. Primary care will be the blazing sun at the centre; hospitals will occupy the outermost orbit.

In the earlier days of Canadian medicare, most funding went to hospitals. As a result, many types of care that had traditionally taken place in the community shifted to hospitals, where they would be covered. Needless to say during the recent cutbacks the hospital podiatrists and psychologists were the first to be let go. They are every bit as necessary, but they are now back in the community and part of the ever-increasing privately funded sector of health care.

This new health care solar system simply recognizes what is already happening. Most health care already takes place at the primary-care level. And the hospital share of total health care spending is steadily shrinking as the non-hospital share grows. Surely it should be obvious that the family practice belongs at the centre of this new alignment. Not that hospitals will become any less professional or essential. For the one person in a thousand who ends up in a so-called tertiary-care hospital every year, these institutions must function as vital parts of a fully integrated health care system that is designed for the other 999.

The key to the successful integration of hospitals into a reformed system is the family doctor as playing coach. The family doctor will always have at least courtesy privileges at the local hospital—which means he or she can always walk onto the ward and get access to a patient's chart—and will *always* be expected to provide support for a patient's care during a hospital stay. It simply makes common sense that a patient's primary physician, the person who knows the medical history and the family history better than anyone else, should coach the patient through each and every hospital stay and through every aspect of his or her health care experience.

Many times, upon reading a patient's hospital chart, I was able to correct the errors in a history taken by a medical student. Occasionally I caught the same error in the consultation note written by a resident who had obviously not taken the history personally but had relied upon an erroneous admitting history. This is one of the ways family doctors can be helpful, even in big teaching hospitals.

When the hospital physician is the bearer of bad news, the family doctor can be especially helpful. For one thing, the family doctor knows the patient and how best to break the news. For another—and this happens all the time—a patient often goes into shock upon hearing a word like *cancer* and so doesn't get the whole message. The family doctor can make sure that, once the shock has passed, the patient gets the complete story.

The biggest and richest hospitals—the university-affiliated teaching hospitals—aren't going to like this fundamental change in values or the shift in status it implies. They are used to thinking of themselves as the elite and tend to operate on the assumption that every other part of the system is there to serve them. This is why many family physicians gravitate to smaller, more community-oriented hospitals, places where a patient-centred approach to hospital care is already closer to reality.

Many hospitals and their leaders will almost certainly resist a system where they no longer occupy the centre. But once they get used to it, they'll actually find that they like it. It's more satisfying to work on a team and to be paid for giving the very best care possible to those who actually need a specialist's level of care. The bad referrals by family physicians who dump difficult patients diminish once there is a real working relationship between family doctors and hospital specialists. A patient of mine, who was a family physician herself, once expressed astonishment that the specialists at Women's College would call me back and that I knew them and they knew me. At her much larger hospital that wasn't the case. The Women's College model can become the norm if we create integrated teams of family doctors and specialists who work together. The widespread practice of "shared care," in which family physicians and specialists work together on obstetrical and psychiatric cases, is a good beginning. Of course, with the family physician always at the intersection of the lines of communication, fewer patients will end up in hospital in the first place.

And that's part of the point. The writing is on the wall for the elite teaching hospital as a law unto itself, for the huge, faceless, monolithic mega hospital where family doctors are ignored and patients are treated at the convenience of doctors and nurses and administrators. I find it extremely disappointing that the recent trend towards amalgamating smaller hospitals into huge health care consortiums swims in the opposite direction from the most knowledgeable and enlightened reform thinking.

A healthier system for all of us

There you have it, my vision for meaningful health care reform, reform that gives the patient both power and responsibility. As I hope I've already made clear, my vision is of a system so fully integrated that each part can be said to be doing its job only when it keeps the rest of the system in the loop, when the whole health care system functions like a team. Such a degree of integration will soon be made easier by recent developments in communication technology that can give the patient and his or her family physician access to all the information they need at the punch of a computer key or the swipe of a health card. (The electronic medical record, or EMR, is discussed in chapter 8.)

It is important to point out, however, that making the system sustainable means addressing the more deep-rooted health problems in our society, the so-called social determinants of health. Primary among these must be the continuing problem of poverty in our country. But there are many others: domestic violence and on-the-job stress; environmental pollution; workplace and traffic safety; and the causes of drug and alcohol addiction. Until we attack such problems at their root, the health care system will continue to face serious challenges on the demand side.

The Plan

Getting at the social determinants of health must be part of our approach to better public health policy. And better public health policy means a greater emphasis on disease prevention and health promotion. I believe that the reformed system, which will make information more readily available and the tracking of disease patterns in the population so much easier, will contribute enormously to improved public health. This in turn will mean healthier Canadians and less stress on the health care system. Although I sometimes sound like a walking, talking advertisement for family physicians, I must add here that family doctors are the physicians who know the most about the social determinants of health. They see patients every day whose real problems stem from the circumstances of their lives, not from genes or germs.

Is such a system really attainable and attainable soon? Absolutely. Will it cost the moon? Absolutely not. In the rest of this final section of the book, I look in more detail at the evidence that indicates how well the new system can ultimately work and how much money it can save. The concluding chapter turns to the political realm—the realm of citizen advocacy and citizen action and the future roles of the federal and provincial governments in concert with all the "stakeholders," the various professional groups representing those who actually work inside the health care system. Whatever governments propose, the individual Canadian is the ultimate arbiter. Successful reform of Canadian health care won't happen without the commitment of the Canadian public. Knowledgeable patients will be the catalyst of change.

Poll after poll continues to show that Canadians believe in universal health care and don't want to start down the slippery slope of privatization. They may be worried about how

well the system is serving them and where it is heading—
about the obvious problems it is experiencing and the signs
of deterioration—but they don't want to lose it. Canadians
are our best hope for the future of universal health care.

8

We Already Have the Tools

Community health clinics (CLSCs in Quebec) have broad support across the country. Shirley Douglas, Tommy Douglas's daughter and an indefatigable champion of health reform, and the Canadian Health Coalition are great believers in expanding this model, hopefully to all Canadians. However, there are a lot of physicians in private practices with long office leases. How do we start these doctors along the road to reform? How can we ensure that all community health clinics provide twenty-four-hour care?

The Chatham experiment

In spring, 2000, Dr. Brian Gamble and a group of a dozen other family physicians in Chatham, Ontario, launched a "clustering" pilot project, a group practice that provides comprehensive care to roughly 24,000 patients and is available for telephone advice twenty-four hours a day, seven days a week. Similar pilot clusters have recently started up at six other sites in Ontario: Paris, Kingston, Hamilton, Ottawa, Thunder Bay, and Parry Sound. In all, these pilot projects, funded jointly by the federal and provincial governments and established under the auspices of the Ontario Medical Association, involve around 200 doctors and serve approximately 450,000 patients.

In the Chatham cluster, all the doctors have retained their separate offices, but they've pooled their resources so that one night in every ten or twelve one of the doctors is on overnight call. A patient can reach this doctor by phoning an answering service that then pages him or her. When the cluster is fully operational, it will allow for extended office hours and the sharing of patient records between physicians. Relevant parts of the patient's record will also be available to the local pharmacist and at the local hospital emergency room. Thus, whether a patient reaches his or her own doctor, or another of the cluster's physicians who's on call, he or she will get the best care possible.

Each patient who agrees to be part of Brian Gamble's roster signs a contract agreeing that he is their primary-care doctor and giving him permission to share his or her medical history and such records as immunization schedules with the other doctors in the cluster. At the moment, Gamble is still paid on a fee-for-service basis for each patient on his roster, up to an agreed maximum amount per patient per month, but several of the other Ontario pilot clusters are experimenting with a pure rostering model, where the government pays the practice for the total number of patients it looks after, regardless of how many billable services it provides. These practices can divide up this total amount as they see fit, in effect paying each employee a monthly salary.

Gamble would prefer to be part of one of these "global" clusters. He has never liked what he refers to as the "treadmill" of fee for service. "I would like more time to practise preventive medicine," he says, "and more time for evidence-based medicine." But he is excited about the Chatham pilot and believes clustering, or group practice, points the way to the future. It has already cut his paperwork and made him feel like a better doctor. "I feel we may be on the cutting edge here. We want to see if we can feel better, our patients can feel better and our system works better."

Gamble foresees the day when most, if not all, Ontario family physicians will be practising in groups, some in virtual clusters like his own, others sharing the same office space. These group practices will take advantage of the latest in information technology to provide the best medicine in the world. Soon he expects to have access to his patients' records via his laptop. Whether he's in his office or on call, he'll thus be able to pull up the information he needs instantly.

But he also recognizes that many physicians will resist the change. One Saskatchewan doctor he knows told him, "If they force me to roster, I'll just move my office to a third-floor walk-up." By so doing, this physician could cull older and sicker patients from his practice, people who can't or won't climb two flights of stairs. Whatever model we finally come up with must eliminate any opportunity for doctors to cull the more time-consuming or difficult-to-treat patients from their practices, something that now happens all too often under the fee-for-service model. Any family physician with an aging practice knows other doctors who refuse to take on older patients. That's one of the abuses that the rostered group practice is designed to stop. As Gamble puts it, the rostering model allows a group of doctors to "risk share." Since a group of doctors can handle a much larger patient population than can a solo practitioner, it can much more easily take on a varied patient group that includes both lower-risk (less likely to get sick) and higher-risk (more likely to get sick) patients.

Gamble is particularly excited about the potential for improving patient care by means of a sophisticated, continuously updated electronic medical record (EMR). This record would allow him to combine a patient's personal and family history with demographic and other information. Such a comprehensive medical record for each individual patient would hone a doctor's ability to prevent problems before they occur. Furthermore, computer analysis of all the EMRs within a single practice cluster would help it set priorities and identify areas of concern. For example, the analysis might reveal a higher-than-usual risk of heart attack for certain patients or the fact that the practice is way behind in vaccinating its child patients. I know of one practice in Calgary that has a monthly education meeting for different patient groups, diabetics one month, people on blood pressure medication the next month. These meetings can disseminate a lot of information that may prevent unnecessary problems. This is just one example of the sorts of strategies group practices will have the time and money to implement. An EMR would also allow appropriate patients to automatically get notice of such meetings.

Eventually, when work on the human genome is complete, combining EMRs with population health statistics will permit each practice to develop a sophisticated practice profile. Such a profile will also allow the cluster's capitation rate—the amount it is paid for each patient in its care—to be adjusted to reflect the average amount of time its patients need, making it easier to ensure that practices that deal with sicker or more time-consuming patients earn a premium.

Gamble also believes that as part of a fully rostered group practice he will be able to see more patients on average than he does now, while providing even better care. He won't have to examine a patient whom his nurse practitioner can treat as well or better, just because that's the only way he can legally bill for his service. He'll have more information at his fingertips so that he can make a better diagnosis more quickly. And he'll have time to practise more preventive medicine. The cluster's electronically maintained patient record system will remind him how long it's been since he last counselled a heavy smoker to quit, for example.

Brian Gamble's enthusiasm about the Chatham pilot is infectious. It is the enthusiasm of a good family physician for an approach that allows him to practise the profession he loves more effectively. Gamble concludes: "Family doctors enjoy high esteem in the community. Now we'll have time to practise an even better brand of medicine, medicine that makes sense in the twenty-first century."

While it's too soon to judge the success of Ontario's pilot clusters, their success won't come as any surprise to those of us who remember an earlier Ontario experiment in the group-practice model, the health service organization (HSO). When I described this experiment in chapter 4, "The Doctor Is Part of the Solution," I argued that the HSOs shouldn't have failed; they were never given a proper chance to succeed. Walter Rosser, Chair of the Department of Family and Community Medicine at the University of Toronto, agrees. As he puts it, "We already have twenty years of experience with rostering. Rostering works." The few HSOs still operating have been successful in delivering to their patient populations far more comprehensive care than is the norm, providing invaluable experience in medical teamwork on the primary-care front line.

Brian Gamble and the other doctors forming primary-care clusters are building on the experience gained from the HSO experiment to design an even better group-practice model. One of their advantages is the ability to use the latest in the exploding field of information technology. This technology promises to revolutionize not just the individual group practice, but the way the entire health care system works.

The new health care *info*structure

The Ontario clusters are already showing how patient information can be shared within a group practice and with appropriate providers within a local area. But what happens to one of Dr. Gamble's Chatham patients who gets sick during a vacation in British Columbia or the Maritimes? Surely in the age of the Internet, a doctor or a hospital 1,000 or 10,000 kilometres away should be able to get instant access to relevant patient histories—with the patient's consent, of course. That is the goal of those designing the new health information infrastructure, or infostructure, which I view as an essential component of a reformed system. It will not only mean better care, it will enhance the portability of Canadian medicare.

At the first and most obvious level, this infostructure must be set up so that personal medical records can be appropriately shared while individual privacy is protected. Every user of the Canadian health care system needs instant access to relevant records anywhere in Canada—and ultimately anywhere in the world—including a chronological record of all recent medications prescribed and treatments undergone. Your pharmacist or an emergency room doctor, or a family doctor you visit while away from home should, with your consent, have access to the completely up-to-date relevant information, including what medications you are currently taking or the fact that you had an allergic reaction to a particular local anaesthetic once when you had a tooth drilled.

What parts of your personal record should be available? Anything that's relevant to your care. Who decides? You do, in consultation with your coach, the family physician. How will this be made available? There are several models, and it's not clear yet which one will prevail.

The Royal Bank and the province of Manitoba worked on a smart card for years. But it looks like this approach may end up as a non-starter in Canada. It has already been rejected in Quebec and Ontario, and for several very good reasons. It would be simple enough to make the health card you carry in your wallet much smarter. (Right now these cards are just plain stupid.) The original idea was to have a core amount of your health information encoded right on your card. Just as a swipe of your bank credit card and a password allows access to certain information about your account, so a swipe of a smart card could theoretically give access to part of your medical record. Now, there is a recognition that for health care emergencies we shouldn't have to rely on a plastic card that can be lost or stolen and can be damaged so that the magnetized strip on the back doesn't work. We need a more reliable system, one that means a doctor can always treat a patient appropriately, even if that patient is unconscious or the card has been damaged or misplaced.

Ontario is actively looking at the best way of sharing patient information under a program called the "Smart Systems for Health Project." The province is also experimenting with something called the Emergency Health Record. Under this system, in a medical emergency, selected patient information will be made available anywhere in Ontario to any qualified medical professional. In the future, however, a system that selectively permits the whole record to be available with your permission and only parts of it in others will almost certainly come into being.

In Ontario, it appears that access to this information will be gained via a special Internet network run on the public phone lines but to which access is strictly limited. The government will pay to set up the infrastructure so that every physician's office and every hospital is connected via this network to a central server where all patient records are kept.

But what about your privacy? This is a legitimate fear, and safeguarding privacy must be a central concern as we develop information technology for health care.

The technology necessary to protect privacy already exists or is almost here. Encryption techniques were developed in the late 1980s and technology for protecting privacy over large information networks, or Privacy-Enhancement Technology (PET), is now being perfected. Under PET, every patient might be given several pseudo identification numbers along with the real one. His or her medical records might be subdivided into different categories or different levels of access, each separate file available only by means of one specific password. Thus allergy information could be more easily accessible than mental health records. In this way the other parts of the file would automatically be kept from prying eyes. Thus data would be linked to the patient only with the patient's consent. Think of this system as resembling adjoining rooms in a hotel where both parties need to use their key to open the door between them.

The worry that electronic medical records would be cumbersome and time-consuming to maintain—worse than the current paper filing system—doesn't seem to be justified. The job of keeping files up to date and inputting data will be decentralized. It will take place every time a health care provider makes a health care decision: at the lab, the hospital, the pharmacy, or in the doctor's office. The person making the decision will place the data on the patient's electronic computer chart at the time each decision is made.

The Plan

When talking about sharing information electronically, we should remember that privacy has always been an issue when it comes to medical records. And consider the benefits. The electronic record, at the very least, will make it easier to scrutinize the treatment patterns of health care providers, thereby enhancing our ability to identify, for example, poor prescribing habits and to improve them without identifying individual patients.

A health information infrastructure will fit hand and glove with the broader goals of the reformed health care system, making the full integration of the various parts of the system easier and more effective. Gone will be the days when you or an emergency room doctor knew nothing of your previous care and had to start from scratch, or when you or your pharmacist had no way of knowing what other prescriptions you'd recently had filled at the all-night drug store.

Putting this infostructure in place will require more than technical expertise. As with designing the compensation and incentive scheme for rostered practices, designing the infostructure will involve important issues about values and policies. Patients have a long-standing interest in access to their own records, documented by more than one royal commission. Even in a paper system, that access has been less than complete. An electronic system, making the same information potentially available to a number of different health care providers, may well heighten a person's interest in being able to review his or her own health file. Who wants a doctor's unguarded and possibly derogatory or inaccurate assessment circulating widely? And, if the patient is to be the captain of the team, that patient should have access to the same record as the coach and others. In sum, patients should have access to every piece of health information with their name on it.

These interests suggest that patient or consumer involvement will be crucial in designing the electronic records system. Essential, too, will be our experience with other initiatives in portable records, including the Ontario Antenatal Record (currently hard copy) that accompanies each pregnant woman though pregnancy, delivery, and postpartum care. A steady commitment to really involve those with affected interests and relevant knowledge must inform the design and implementation of the new health care infostructure.

More information for better medicine

Up to now, I've considered the implications of electronic systems for the individual patient and his or her caregivers, whether in the hospital or in the community. I've also looked at their benefits to the emerging primary-care model, the group practice, which will use these records to create profiles of its patient population—while keeping individual records confidential—that will allow it to tailor its methods and resources to serve it better. But the ready availability of medical knowledge that these records will make possible represents another major benefit.

The infostructure has the potential to make information about clinical trials, new techniques and treatments, and recent scientific breakthroughs available to patients and doctors more easily and in more detail. The more regularly doctors can gain access to updated information about evidence-based treatments and best practices, the better medicine they'll practise. A fully developed infostructure will also be a huge boon to medical research, providing a two-way information street between physicians on the front lines of treatment and researchers in their laboratories and in the field. Such information-sharing will make doctors and patients better at prevention, once again saving money through the practice of smarter medicine.

Some of the information we need is already being gathered—in the private health sector. David Imrie is the president of Assure Health Management Inc., a company that manages the drug plans for a group of insurance companies whose clients total about 6 million Canadians. He says that private "health insurers" are already using existing data on prescription drug use to "manage" their responsibilities. According to Imrie, prescription drug use provides "an excellent profile of a person's health status." His numbers reveal that a startlingly small 5 per cent of patients account for 40 per cent of drug costs, that 5 per cent of employees account for 50–70 per cent of accident costs.

A computerized patient record can easily include automatic alerts and reminders that tell the family physician when to call a patient in for a PAP smear, a blood pressure check, a birthday physical. Veterinarians and dentists have been doing "recall" reminders for years! With home computers it won't be long before automatic e-mail reminders will be the norm, as well as access to your own medical record and other ongoing communication with the doctor's office and pharmacy, or the home care provider.

Some readers may immediately wonder, "What about people who don't have access to the Internet?" Good question, since equality of access to health information is becoming as important as universal access to medical care. What about people who either can't afford or don't choose to own personal computers, who aren't "on the Web"? I foresee a kiosk in every doctor's office and pharmacy and library branch that's as easy to use as an automatic banking machine. In remote settings, such facilities could be installed in community centres, town halls, or band offices. Perhaps Industry Canada's Community Access Program could be adopted for this purpose. Of course, standards for any public access points are important and must be developed with feedback from the people who will actually be using them.

What Imrie refers to as the new "connectivity" of health information will feed into better public health policy by giving us far better insight into the health of various populations. The most complete information we now collect is based on doctors' billing data. The new health information infostructure will mean we can collect better data and make far better decisions about where to spend our health care dollars.

Finally, you're probably wondering about the cost of all this fancy new technology. It certainly won't come cheap, but the cost will be a one-time investment. The federal government has already invested just under $30 million over 3 years in the creation of a Canadian Health Network designed to "empower the public, strengthen and integrate health care services, and create the information resources for accountability and continuous feedback on factors affecting the health of Canadians." But $30 million is only a drop in the bucket. Once the provinces, territories, and Ottawa agree on a national information strategy, all levels of government will need to invest several billion dollars to create a comprehensive national system. I believe that investment will pay us back many times over.

Models of reform

The new health care infostructure will mean that good news travels faster and good models spread sooner between regions and provinces. Ontario's physician clusters are among a growing number of pilot projects and promising experiments that are paving the way to primary-care reform. In British Columbia, a primary-care reform demonstration project is now completing its first year, testing a system of rostered practices with capitated payments. Early response to this project seems generally positive. One of the participants, a family physician with a practice that includes 200 patients with HIV, comments, "There is less pressure to move patients through quickly. It is easier to take the time to deal with complex problems." In almost every province, primary-care reform is on the front burner.

Especially promising are the early experiments at integrating all the parts of the system so that primary care interacts more efficiently with other levels of care. One of the leaders here is Edmonton's Capital Regional Health Authority, whose success at avoiding the recent emergency room crisis I described in chapter 1.

Integration seems to be progressing faster in provinces that have opted to decentralize their systems into semi-autonomous regional authorities. Such as those in Edmonton and Victoria.

No matter where you look, promising models are sprouting up. Just about every province is investing in better home care. A group of British Columbia nurses now provides after-hours "telecare," offering basic medical advice by telephone. Specialists in the Northwest Territories are already on salary, having decided this is a more efficient system. Toronto's Hospital for Sick Children has launched a TeleHomeCare Project in partnership with Bell Ontario. The project will allow patients who are not acutely ill to go home sooner but have their progress monitored via two-way audio-visual hookup. In a pilot just launched by the

Capital Health Authority in Victoria, British Columbia, copies of *Healthwise*, a self-care manual, were distributed to a test population, and backed up by twenty-four-hour telephone advice by registered nurses. In the months that followed, unnecessary or inappropriate visits to ERs, walk-in clinics, and family physicians were dramatically down. A broader pilot is now under way.

All in all, our problem won't be finding good examples to imitate, but choosing the best of a very good lot. There's absolutely no question in my mind that we have the tools at hand to enact comprehensive health care reform, in terms of both treatment models and new technologies. During the transition there will be some hefty costs, especially as we invest in information systems that connect all health providers and all Canadian citizens into a single interrelated information and feedback web. But these costs are investments in our future and in a system that really works for all of us.

There's one aspect of reform that information technology can foster but that money can't buy: accountability. Perhaps the greatest weakness of Canadian medicare today, and the root cause of much of its human and financial waste, is the almost complete lack of accountability. We must have a system where both administrators and health care providers are held accountable for the quality of service they provide. How we can build accountability throughout a fully integrated health care system is the subject of the next chapter.

9

Building Accountability

It's not safe enough to get sick

Every developed country in the world is grappling with the growing problem of medical error. In the United States, a recent report by the Institute of Medicine (IOM) called for "rigorous changes throughout the health care system" to fix the problem. "The human cost of medical errors is high," the IOM stated. "Based on the findings of one major study, medical errors kill some 44,000 people in U.S. hospitals each year. Another study puts the number much higher, at 98,000. Even using the lower estimate, more people die from medical mistakes each year than from highway accidents, breast cancer, or AIDS." Medical error is "one of the nation's leading causes of death and injury."

Not long ago, the United States Office of Technology Assessment reported that as few as 20 per cent of all medical procedures had been scientifically demonstrated as safe and beneficial. I'd say that's an optimistic assessment. According to Arthur Schafer, who simply articulates what doctors know but don't like to admit to themselves, the current state of medical practice resembles "small islands of [important] knowledge in a sea of ignorance and uncertainty." As long as doctors are afraid to admit when they don't know and work in a culture where they're supposed to be perfect, medical error will remain a threat.

Although no nationwide studies of medical error exist in Canada, there is no reason to think that our system has lower levels than those in the United States. I should point out here that the term *medical error* covers a wide range of occurrences, from a mistake during an operation that leads to serious injury or death, to a family doctor's failure to diagnose an identifiable complaint or a specialist's bad handwriting that causes the pharmacist to dispense the wrong drug. It can be as seemingly innocuous as the failure of a hospital to notify a patient's family physician promptly of the patient's course of medication upon release and as elusive as a mistake in recording a detail on a patient's medical record. It can be a systemic failure like the double prescription for the same drug by a family physician and a specialist who haven't talked to each other.

Medical error will always be with us—as long as medicine is practised by human beings. No one is perfect and no human system functions without flaws. But the current levels of error in health care systems all over the developed world are far too high. Fortunately, they are also unnecessary. It should and can be much safer to get sick, and much safer to deal with any part of the system, however complex and sophisticated the overall system has become.

The people who study hazardous industries, such as the nuclear industry and the airline industry, seem to agree that the more complex a system is the more prone it is to error. This observation makes perfect sense. The more pieces to a puzzle, the more likely that one will go missing. As a recent article in the *Journal of the American Medical Association* put it, "Modern health care presents the most complex safety challenge of any activity on earth."

The experts also point out that most error is not caused by a single individual but is the result of a sequence of small failures in the system. Most "catastrophic events," to use the experts' jargon, are the end result of a series of small mistakes that cascade into one big problem. It follows logically, therefore, that the best way to address the problem of medical error is to make sure that little mistakes are harder to make. And that means better accountability.

Accountability is one of those words that is often abused. Here's what it means to me. In the narrowest sense, it means taking responsibility for your actions. But what if the action or event in question has no single author, or no identifiable authors at all? If an individual makes a mistake, does all of the mistake really belong to this one person, or were many other mistakes involved? If the medical system lets you down, who is responsible?

I ask these questions by way of demonstrating that accountability is the key to any successful redesign of our health care system. As health law professor Colleen Flood put it in a recent paper in *Policy Options*, "Improving accountability is key to ensuring Medicare's long-term sustainability. Improving accountability is vital for the simple reason that all systems, when faced with the imperative to contain costs, have strong tendencies to shift costs rather than improve performance." To be effective, accountability must operate at every level and in every part of our system. We have a long way to go before we reach that goal.

Medical accountability in Canada

In Part One of this book, I used a very graphic analogy to highlight the frequency of error in the Canadian medical system. I stated that if our rate of mistakes was transferred to another high-risk business, the North American airline industry, you would see a 747 falling out of the sky every week. The airline comparison points up just how serious the problem is and how much money, as well as human suffering, it costs us. It also makes our failure to deal with this issue inexcusable. In no other high-risk business would such high levels of error be acceptable.

Canadian medicare ought to be able to deliver the safest medicine in the world because our system is one of the simplest, the only system that is delivered to most of the people most of the time in a single tier of services from providers. Canada is the only place in the developed world where most health care is funded by a single payer—the taxpayer—via the two levels of government. Since I believe that the reforms this book proposes will make the system more integrated, they hold out the promise of reducing medical error to the absolute minimum.

One of the main reasons that the airline industry has grown safer over the last few decades, despite the ever more crowded skies, is that regulating authorities have insisted on accountability. If a mistake happens in the air or on the ground, anyone who observes the mistake is duty bound to report it. A pilot doesn't lose his or her job for making a mistake, but only for failing to report one. Such a reporting system can work only if self-reporting doesn't automatically trigger blame. It must be safe for someone to blow the whistle or for an individual to admit committing an error. Only then can a system learn from its mistakes and avoid them in the future.

In Canada, as in the United States, physicians have no incentive to report their mistakes. Just the opposite. Doctors are afraid of being sued for malpractice if they admit they've messed up. Interestingly, the evidence actually shows that malpractice suits involving doctors who immediately admit their mistakes get much smaller awards than those in which the doctor attempted to hide them. The fear of being sued causes doctors to keep their mistakes secret. Legal liability for physician error is the enemy of accountability. The only people it benefits are lawyers and sellers of insurance.

This problem is not confined to physicians. Many professionals live with similar fears about reporting errors, and for similar reasons: fear of court action or professional discipline. For these professionals fear of being punished or actually losing their jobs creates a further deterrent to admitting their mistakes. This is why Judge Horace Krever recommended a no-fault blood system for Canada.

The culture of fear in which doctors and many other professionals operate is created in part by the crime-and-punishment nature of professional regulatory systems. Most professions have self-regulating bodies that mainly respond to complaints from clients or third parties. Not surprisingly, these regulators discipline only the comparatively severe cases of misconduct or failure to meet established standards. As a result, most problems that consumers have with doctors, lawyers, architects, dentists, or building contractors—poor communication, bad attitudes, substandard service—fall below the disciplinary radar.

Yet any complaint made to any regulator, successful or not, requires the expenditure of time and resources and causes aggravation to all parties. The complaints process means annoying "red tape" for the client, the arbitrator, and the professional. The cumbersome nature of the complaints process becomes yet another deterrent to reporting error.

In addition to self-regulation by professional bodies, we regulate professional activity through the legal system by means of the malpractice action. Any consumer who undertakes such an action, however, is once again in for a long process with an uncertain outcome. Any doctor who gets sued is in for an equally long haul. No wonder physicians bend over backwards to avoid any chance of being sued for malpractice. Not only are they highly unlikely to admit mistakes, they may be tempted to order unnecessary tests just because the patient asks for them. Or they may fall back on "tried and true" methods of treatment even when they are fully aware of the evidence for alternatives, especially if these evidence-based alternatives are unconventional.

These two traditional accountability mechanisms cause untold aggravation for consumers and professionals, absorb huge resources of time and money, and yet catch only a tiny fraction of the multitude of slip-ups large and small that occur within our medical system. Perhaps regular recertification and regular performance audits will work better than our largely complaints-based system. And even when an individual or institution is found "guilty" of committing some serious medical error, it may take a very long while for the system to learn the clinical or practice "lesson." All in all, our traditional methods of accountability leave a lot to be desired.

Dr. Patrick McNamara of the College of Physicians and Surgeons of Ontario, the body that regulates the province's doctors, worries that "we have no mechanism to deal adequately with problems caused by system failure." What do we do about the infection created when a patient is discharged without appropriate home care and the nurse never arrives to remove the drain from the wound? What do we do when the hospital "forgets" to call back a person treated for a mild heart attack, then released on the understanding that a stress cardiogram would be done within two weeks? More dramatically, who is responsible when the ambulance transporting a patient with a severe asthma attack can't find a local emergency room open to take him to and he dies on the way to a more distant hospital? Who gets to decide when to place the emergency room on "ambulance redirect"? Is that whole policy an error? Who is accountable?

As the airline example proves, there is a better way than a complaints-based system where many errors fall through the cracks and where there is no system-wide incentive to report error. This better way is to build accountability into every stage of the health care process, between physician and patient, between specialist and general practitioner, between members of various health care professions, and on the part of hospital or clinic administrators who are responsible for employed staff. As the editors of the *Journal of the American Medical Association* put it, "Traditionally, error analysis has focused on people as unreliable components. However, the new look has focused research on how people, individually, as groups, and as organizations, make safety." In a system where everyone has an incentive to identify or admit mistakes and work at preventing similar mistakes from happening, safety increases exponentially, as a number of test projects have shown.

Since 1987 the state of Massachusetts has required each of its health care facilities, from hospitals to family practices, to establish a Patient Care Assessment system. Hospitals resisted the program most strongly, but have now accepted it because it works. Safety is up, complaints are down, and the typical hospital oversight committee functions with only three staff members and three board members. The health management organizations (HMOs) in the United States have developed a computerized patient satisfaction survey with thirty-six questions designed to elicit the patient's positive and negative experiences with the system. Today, Canada's Hospital Accreditation system has moved to a patient-centred model. Hopefully Ontario's new hospital report cards will begin the process of better accountability and transparency.

It has often been suggested that we should give every user of our system a cost statement covering their use of the health care system during the year. Why would it be important to know exactly how much our personal health care costs? Some people fear such individual cost accounting will make those who pay higher taxes complain that they aren't getting their money's worth. They also fear that seeing the numbers will cause some others to use the system more, but I don't think either of these fears is legitimate. An annual cost accounting helps citizens understand how much value they are getting from their system. More likely it will encourage patients to use the system more wisely. Finally, it can become an important part of making the system transparent to all its users.

Transparency is another one of those buzzwords whose meanings sometimes get blurred from overuse. If our health care system becomes transparent, then we can "see through it." In other words, what people are doing and how they are doing is out in the open for everyone to see. If it's transparent it automatically becomes more accountable. I learned how effective this sort of transparency can be when I worked in Australia in the late 1970s. At each visit to the doctor, pensioners and those on welfare signed a form that recorded, item by item, his or her medical expenditures. Australian patients knew their health care wasn't free.

Continuous quality improvement can happen only in a climate where it pays to report your mistakes and where good performance is rewarded. One of my teachers, the late Dr. Irwin Bean, used a memorable phrase to explain why mediocre physicians often have very successful practices: These are the doctors "who practise bad medicine charmingly." With no way of rating a doctor's performance, patients can more easily be taken in by charmingly bad medicine.

The Plan

If we don't build system-wide accountability into a reformed Canadian health care system, many of the advantages of reform will be lost. Accountability is essential not only to increasing safety for users, but also to making a fully integrated system possible.

Building accountability

The first question you might reasonably ask is: "Accountability to whom?" My answer won't surprise anyone who's read this far: first and last, to the patient. In a patient-centred system of accountability, every health care outcome would be measured or rated on the basis of how well it served the patient, the ultimate recipient of every health care transaction. But accountability flows in every direction and benefits every person who provides care, from family doctors, nurses, and pharmacists, to hospital emergency room personnel.

The next question follows naturally: "Accountability by whom?" The simple answer is: by everyone. It's easy to focus our worries on doctors, above all the surgeons who perform at the riskiest frontier of medicine. We've all heard horror stories of botched operations, lethal doses of medication administered in error, diagnoses getting mixed up with fatal results. But these represent only the tip of the error iceberg.

Since high-profile errors are almost always the end result of many small system failures, the only way to reduce individual mishaps is to make every single person who works in the health care system accountable to every person he or she connects with at every level. Such an approach is the surest route to system-wide accountability.

The final question is this: "Accountability for what?" To

quote a recent Health Canada document, "accountability involves assessing outcomes against some pre-determined expectations of what the health system should be providing to Canadians." In other words, accountability means measuring quality against established standards.

Many good ideas for injecting accountability into the Canadian health care system have been put forward. Common to all of them is coming up with a meaningful set of standards against which the health care system will be measured. Such standards do not come ready made. Choosing the standards will involve reaching consensus about what are the health and service goals most important to Canadians. Health goals for the whole country can be very general, like increasing life expectancy or lowering infant mortality, or quite specific, for example, reasonable hysterectomy rates. They might target, for example, outcomes for certain demographic groups or with respect to certain conditions or procedures—for example, diabetes in aboriginal people—or compare bypass surgery rates between men and women. Our health care standards can encompass not just medical treatments and practices, but also quality of service and levels of customer satisfaction. It can make access to 24/7 primary care a national benchmark.

At this stage in the evolution of Canada's health care system, there is no established body poised to develop these standards. In my opinion, the process for developing them—including figuring out who will do the developing—is one of the essential components of health care reform. Articulating values, exploring priorities, and successfully synthesizing clinical research with consumer expectations are all complex undertakings. These activities require balancing and judgement. They require an inclusive process, with adequate representation from all stakeholders.

And they require time. It is not enough for some elite group to hatch a set of instant standards of health care and then say to Canadians, "Take them or leave them." Canadians do not like to be dealt with in this way, as the failures of the Meech Lake and Charlottetown constitutional accords have shown. We need to start this process now, so that the detailed work of achieving consensus can take place.

Although Canada does not currently have an overarching health standards body equivalent to the International Standards Organization (ISO), which sets standards for manufacturing and service industries, we do have much accumulated wisdom and a great deal of expertise on which to draw. And we have a rich variety of knowledgeable consumer groups well able to articulate patients' interests in treatment and service.

Various medical specialties have begun to develop "clinical guidelines" for various conditions and have agreed on indications when certain interventions are appropriate. At first, individual doctors tend to resist such guidelines, fearing they will restrict their freedom to practise, but once such guidelines are in place, they inevitably prove extremely effective. When I sat on the Ontario government's first Consensus Panel on Anti-Infectives, there was a great deal of initial scepticism. Many thought our little manual would be rejected by the profession. Instead, it was an overwhelming success. Doctors loved this version of one-stop shopping for cost effectiveness that documented support not only for prescribing the best drug, but also for cheaper drugs, when these drugs have proved just as effective.

When patients are privy to clinical guidelines, good things happen. Take, for example, the Ottawa Ankle Rules, consensus guidelines developed at the Ottawa Hospital on how to treat ankle injuries. According to these guidelines only ankle injuries accompanied by swelling, bruising, and inability to bear weight need an x-ray. The rest, mostly sprained ankles, need RICE (rest, ice, compression, elevation). Patients who know the rules don't insist on x-rays they don't need. If days later the ankle isn't behaving like a sprain, an x-ray would then be done. But hundreds of unnecessary x-rays would be spared.

The converse is also true. Patients who know the rules can remind the doctor or the hospital when appropriate medication has gotten lost in the shuffle. Patients leaving hospital after treatment for a heart attack ought to know to insist on being released with a prescription for a beta blocker and to take an aspirin once a day, medications that can prevent a recurrence.

We are just beginning to get better numbers on waiting lists for high-demand procedures. These will help all the health care stakeholders, including patients, determine acceptable waiting times for different tests or procedures. Similarly, we need report cards on individual hospitals, group practices, nursing homes, home care deliverers—and hospital departments. To work, these report cards must move beyond blame to become progress reports on a system constantly striving to get better. Effective report cards will be designed not just to measure the quality of outcomes, but to help providers learn from mistakes, prevent future mistakes, and improve overall quality.

No matter what methods and mechanisms we choose for building accountability, we must be able to measure outcomes and monitor quality. We have already made a start in this direction by using billing codes to track information province by province. The data aren't perfect, but even looking at patterns of surgical intervention has already proved quite telling. For instance, the frequency of

Caesarean section, hospital by hospital, has allowed "evidence-based" researchers to pinpoint the hospitals with the lowest rates, whose best practices are worth emulating. By studying the hospitals with the lowest Caesarean section rates, Ellen Hodnett was able to demonstrate that they all had two things in common: a one-to-one nurse–patient ratio and doctors and nurses that liked each other! Saving dollars on staffing clearly increases costs on the need for surgical intervention and severely changes the quality of those first few days as a mother. The billing data also show that the hysterectomy rate in some cities is three times greater than the average. If a woman living in North Bay knows that the local hysterectomy rate is three times the Toronto average, she's likely to ask her gynecologist some very probing questions.

Creating a comprehensive monitoring system won't be easy, but we already have the technical tools to make one possible. No matter how perfect the technology, however, a system is only as good as the standards it uses for its benchmarks. That's where the toughest work will lie: in the political realm. Nor will we ever achieve a perfect set of health care standards. In fact, the evolving nature of medical research and treatment practice means that any set of standards will always be a work in progress, continuously refined and improved. First and soonest, we need to agree on a core set of principles and a basic set of standards.

The accountability process can and must operate at many different levels. On a national or provincial basis, we may choose to establish some form of health care auditor who, together with an advisory council of citizens, can keep an eye on the big picture and monitor how the system as a whole is doing: how efficiently we are using our health care dollars and how successfully we are achieving good outcomes. In individual sectors—hospitals, primary care, nursing homes, etc.—accountability may focus on the idea of a "report card"—a regular report on how well a particular sector, or even a particular institution or practice within a sector, is doing. Any such report card must be instantly and immediately accessible to all health care consumers. As Monique Bégin recently argued, "The system needs incentive mechanisms to promote reform. Hospitals that can demonstrate improved results because of evidence-based best practices while controlling their budgets should be rewarded by their province or regional health authority."

What difference will report cards make? For one thing, they will support, even encourage, consumer advocacy. Combined with the information available through an expanding health infostructure (see chapter 8), report cards will give consumers the information they need to insist on high-quality care. Waiting lists are an excellent example of the need for consistency and accuracy in reporting. It was clear in the alarming Fraser Institute report on waiting lists that the same patient was often on the list for more than one surgeon. This meant that the estimated "wait time" was grossly exaggerated because, once a procedure was done, some patients disappeared from as many as five different lists. Many provinces have moved to a "first available bank teller" approach that accurately reflects the real number of people waiting for a specific procedure. Any measurement we design must tell the real story.

Denying a patient the optimal treatment because it is too expensive, or simply not mentioning it at all, would stop under a system where clinical guidelines were in the public domain. I have long felt that it was wrong for rural patients to be offered traditional gall bladder surgery that requires at least six weeks off work, without being given the option to have laparoscopic gall bladder surgery in a city hospital, which only requires a few days off. Surely that decision should be up to the patient.

For report cards to be effective, though, they must not simply assign blame. They must not just measure the quality of outcomes but also help providers learn from their mistakes so that overall quality can be improved. Such report cards, aimed at continuous improvement, not blame, will contribute to an overall culture of accountability where there will be rewards for improvement and recognition of outstanding achievement.

How might more accountability ease our current problem with waiting lists for certain treatments and procedures? In a health care system accountable to its users, waiting lists would become patient-centred: those most in need as opposed to those first in line would have priority. The system at the Queen Elizabeth Hospital in Halifax seems to be working well. There, a patient's place on the waiting list for heart surgery is regularly reviewed by the cardiac team, which moves the most urgent cases to the top of the list. A rural heart attack victim shouldn't have to wait six weeks to see an urban cardiologist, another two for an angiogram, and another two for an appointment with the cardiovascular surgeon—only then to be placed on the waiting list for heart surgery. The Canadian Standards Association has established acceptable management and manufacturing practices for industry. Those companies who've met the benchmarks set by the International Standards Organization can display the ISO seal of approval at their plant and on their company publications. Maybe we need an ISO approach to waiting lists, a national standard by which they're measured, and a panel including consumer representatives that would determine an acceptable wait time for a given procedure.

However we ultimately decide to build accountability, the basic features of a sound system are openness, transparency, measurability, probity, clarity of roles and responsibilities, credibility, objectivity, responsiveness, and a willingness to learn from experience.

As our reformed health care system becomes more integrated—more of a team and less a system of solitudes—higher and higher levels of accountability become possible. The vast majority of complaints are directed at physicians practising alone—without the ongoing peer support that's an automatic feature of the group model. Simply moving from a world of mostly solo practitioners towards an increasing number of group practices will reduce the number of complaints patients now make about their doctors. That is one of the reasons I believe that the group practice—especially of family physicians—should be at the hub of our reformed health care system.

Accountability in a group practice

Just how would this overall regime of health care accountability function at the level of the group practice of family physicians? How would it operate within an individual practice? And how would it play out in terms of the way the practice relates to other parts of the system? Many of the details have yet to be worked out, but lots of good ideas are already in the air.

For starters, in the words of Walter Rosser and Jan Kaperski of the Ontario College of Family Physicians, every family doctor "should be an active staff member of his or her local hospital." Not only does such a relationship cement the connection between the two levels of care and ensure that the doctor can properly play the role of coach, it automatically puts family physicians, whether in solo or group practices, in regular contact with their peers. Under a regional health authority model, a small committee, representative of the various players, might take on the role of setting and monitoring quality standards.

Within the group practice itself, weekly quality-care rounds would be the norm. A clear reporting process for patients and providers would clarify roles and enhance communication. One doctor will likely take on a specific accountability role. If a patient is unhappy about an experience with the practice, he or she must feel safe in reporting such an experience. If one doctor in the practice observes a mistake or commits an error, reporting this mistake must automatically become part of his or her job description. The point of the exercise is neither blame nor punishment, but rather positive feedback that improves quality and prevents a mistake from happening twice.

Race for the top

David Naylor suggests that we need to create a Health Care Performance Pool, a special fund that would reward creativity and innovation. Perhaps we should hand out annual awards to the top performers in health care that will get as much media attention as the Order of Canada. Regardless of the mechanism we choose, our accountability system should be designed to encourage competition to provide the best, the highest quality and the most cost-effective care, not the cheapest. The star programs in every province and every sector ought to be celebrated and emulated.

This approach to health care performance is sometimes called "the race for the top." I look forward to the day sometime soon when health care providers from coast to coast will be vying for the best of the best awards in health delivery, competing for dollars from the Performance Pool and kudos from their peers. When every health care provider is striving to be the best of the best.

As with successful reform of the health care system as a whole, the ultimate guarantee of accountability—of safer and more cost-effective medicine—is the informed patient. As information increases and the system becomes more transparent, accountability skyrockets. When in doubt, give the patient more information, not less, more accessibility, not less, more transparency, not less. I believe doctors have nothing to fear and much to gain from building a more accountable system. Not only will their jobs become less stressful and more rewarding, they may actually end up earning more. In the long run, increasing accountability will reduce errors and make doctors more efficient, thereby saving the system money and making it possible to pay individual doctors more for participating in the accountability process.

The road to accountability runs right alongside the road to reform. Both are paved with shared information and crowded with cars that have patients in the drivers' seats. Accountability is the final ingredient in my recipe for reforming health care without making it cost more.

10

Can We Afford This System?

Throwing money at the problem is not the answer

During the debate over health care funding that followed the March 2000 federal budget, it must have seemed to many Canadians that the only thing the provinces and the federal government could agree on was that the other level of government was at fault. The budget earmarked another $2.5 billion for the provinces to spend on health care, in addition to the $11.5 billion provided the previous year. The provinces retorted that this was way too little, too late—a drop in the bottomless bucket of the rising costs of modern medicine.

There is no question that there are new cost drivers in the system, legitimate concerns about the escalating costs of new and innovative medical technologies, about new and expensive drug therapies. But I'm convinced that such improvements won't necessarily cost more in the long run. Laparoscopic surgery has meant that patients can go home the same day; lots of new technologies have resulted in safer, less invasive procedures. Drugs have meant increased quality of life, particularly for those with emotional and mental illness, allowing them to be productive citizens again. Getting people back to work faster can be a huge benefit to the overall productivity of the country. Just ask

any Workers' Compensation Board how costly long waiting lists are when they are also responsible for replacing
salary out of the same pot until the patient gets the surgery
and can get back to work. We need to stop doing some of
the old procedures and using some of the old drugs. Costs
are additive only if we don't have strategies for getting
practitioners to move to the newer ways of doing things.
We have to put our accountability results into action.

The squabble over dollars has overshadowed the more
pressing need to promote cost-effective practice and evaluate outcomes. It distracts our attention from the more
fundamental questions about how best to reorganize and
integrate the health care system. Boasting about how much
we're spending on health care leads to a shell game that
simply slips spending from one budget to another. If funding for homes for the aged moves from the social services
budget to the health care budget, does that mean we're
spending more on health this year?

People are fed up with the political wrangling over health
care between Ottawa and the provinces. They see through
the political posturing and want action. But they are
confused about just how much more money the system
needs. My answer: In the long term, taking into account
inflation, probably not much more than we're spending
now; in the short term, some major one-time investments.

Lack of money is not the major—or even a major—problem with our health care system, as the latest WHO study
reaffirmed. Canada now spends 9.3 per cent of its gross
national product on health care, making it one of the
biggest spenders in the developed world. Our per capita
spending on health puts us in the top ten countries. There
may be some areas, especially information technology or
the development of better accountability mechanisms,

where we need to make a hefty investment now in order to promote efficiencies down the road. We already spend a great deal of money on health care. Our first priority right now should be to spend that money more wisely. A properly reformed system may not cost much more per capita in real dollars than our system does today. A system reformed along the lines I've described will enable us to see just what we are getting in return for our health care dollars. It will allow us to maximize our return on our national investment in health.

Where will the savings come from?

Under the plan for reform that I've outlined in this final part of the book, there is a huge potential for financial savings. The savings will come from eliminating much of the waste and duplication in our outmoded current system by way of improved organization, better communication, and enhanced accountability: a better integrated system. I've previously mentioned many of the specific areas where we should expect savings to occur.

Here's a summary of how the reformed system will save money.

1. An integrated, patient-centred system will use resources more efficiently.

The system towards which we are moving reverses the traditional top-down model of health care delivery; it builds from the bottom up. The firm and broad foundation of the new health care pyramid is excellent primary care delivered by group practices of family doctors fully integrated with the other aspects of primary care—home care, community clinics, nursing homes, and so on. As every student of health care economics will tell you, primary care is cheaper and more efficient than other levels of care. Each step up the pyramid of health care costs more. By simply placing the emphasis of the new system on primary care delivered as comprehensively and efficiently as possible, we will get more health care in return for every dollar we spend.

2. **Patients will use the system more wisely and efficiently.**

The principle at the heart of the best possible primary care is putting the patient and the family doctor at the centre, the one point in the system to which everything else must relate. I've used the analogy of the patient as captain of the health care team and the doctor as playing coach to highlight the important symbiosis between these two key players. With the primary-care physician in the coaching role, the patient's use of the more expensive levels of care inevitably becomes more selective, more appropriate, and less costly and is accompanied by fewer negative side effects. An informed, respected patient will be the best possible arbiter of front-line accountability.

3. **The new primary-care team will save us money.**

Replacing the fee-for-service payment model with one that rewards quality instead of quantity will mean that healthy incentives replace perverse ones. With the incentives in the right place, each dollar we pay physicians will go farther. Our health care dollars will go farthest where they already count the most: in primary care.

4. **The new health care infostructure will save money in the long run.**

Major savings will ultimately flow from the creation of a sophisticated health care infostructure. Here's just one example of the kinds of savings possible when information is very readily available. As I noted in chapter 2, Canadians spend $7.5 billion yearly on medication that is either wrongly prescribed or improperly taken. With a health care infostructure in place that includes electronic patient records, this costly and harmful situation can and should disappear. I can think of all sorts of better things to do with that $7.5 billion than patching up the system's costly mistakes.

5. **More accountability means more cost-effective medicine.**
Increased accountability will yield healthy savings. Once we've designed a system-wide regime of accountability and created a culture of openness and transparency where admitting mistakes is part of best practices, where monitoring quality is seen as a chance to learn from our mistakes not hide them, better and cheaper medicine will necessarily result. If 30 to 40 per cent of all health services are now dispensed inappropriately, we can save millions of dollars by creating incentives to use our resources more efficiently. A 1995 synthesis report from Queen's University and the University of Ottawa, *Sustainable Health Care for Canada*, developed a "Resource Allocation Framework" that if implemented could translate into savings of about $7 billion annually. The paper suggests that Canada should "create a new set of incentives that will realistically encourage both the providers and patients to choose less costly—but equally effective—health alternatives," the essence of sustainable health care. That $7 billion figure may now be unrealistic—it was based on 1990 data—but substantial savings are certainly possible by making more cost-effective health care choices.

6. Investing in prevention saves money.

Investing in prevention addresses the demand-side of health care: the better we are at preventing illness, the less stress on sickness care, which is by far the most expensive part of our health care system. Here, health care overlaps social determinants. For example, taking even firmer steps to reduce smoking among young people pays big dividends in the long run—preventing heart disease, lung disease, and cancer—and in the short term. Recent California data show a dramatic and almost immediate decrease in health care costs as the smoking rate declines, from premature babies to post-operative pneumonia.

Examples of cost-saving through prevention abound. Think of bicycle helmets, seat belts, the simple use of sunscreen. The Canadian Multicentre Osteoporosis Study showed that regular screening for osteoporosis—to prevent hip fractures in elderly people—would be extremely cost effective. A nonprofit organization called SMARTRISK, founded by pediatric heart surgeon Robert Conn, has undertaken a national program to educate young people about the nine out of ten injuries that are preventable. An unconscionable number of workplace injuries can also be prevented.

Dr. Terry Kavanagh of the Toronto Rehabilitation Institute dramatically disproved the idea that patients who had had a heart attack should rest as "cardiac cripples" for the rest of their life. He demonstrated that regular aerobic exercise enhanced the heart's ability to build durable blood vessel detours around the coronary arteries. In fact many of his post–heart attack patients have run the Boston marathon. The terrible tragedy of fetal alcohol syndrome has consequences way beyond our health care system, from drug addiction to our correctional system (70 per cent of young offenders suffer from either fetal alcohol syndrome or a learning disability or both). We can't afford not to be doing everything in our power to prevent it. In mental health, childhood sexual abuse is responsible for large numbers of women in detox and homeless shelters. Early identification and a society where children can feel safe reporting it can lead to early intervention and much healthier lives.

And I can think of all sorts of things that haven't been tried but that could prevent both illness and expense. How about something as simple as public education to tell seniors how often scatter rugs or stray newspapers on the floor cause hip fractures? For years it has been well known that folic acid in the diet of women before and during their pregnancies can prevent spina bifida and other neurological conditions. For years pediatricians have been calling for the addition of folic acid to flour, just as salt is now iodized so as to prevent thyroid problems. There is no excuse for not taking such preventive measures when we know they will be effective. Other preventive measures won't be as cheap or easy to adopt. In 1978, 2.5 per cent of children had asthma. Today, the figure is 12 per cent. The increase in air pollution in our major cities, second-hand smoke, alterations in the immune system by increased use of antibiotics may all play a role. Governments are moving to reduce automobile emissions and other sources of pollution, but not fast enough. Even the British American Tobacco Company is now warning smokers not to smoke in the presence of children. We need research on the effect of pesticides on learning disabilities and other health problems. We can no longer avert our eyes from the five to ten times greater concentrations of PCBs in the breastmilk of Inuit women than among other Canadian women. A recent OMA study, The Illness Costs of Air Pollution in Ontario, reported that the annual effects of air pollution in Ontario include: 1,920 deaths, up from 1,800 estimated two years earlier; 9,800 hospital admissions; 13,000 emergency room visits; 47 million lost work days. "All of this could be prevented if we had clean air," the report concluded.

There you have it in both specific and general terms: the impressive potential for savings as we move towards the new system. The only way I can see these savings failing to materialize is if we don't take the logic of reform the whole way. If we resort to half-measures, we'll continue to have a health care system that is overfed and undernourished.

Why privatization would cost us money

Proponents of more privately owned health care services in Canada repeat the mindless mantra that only free market forces promote economic efficiency. The *National Post* recently complained that Bill 11, Alberta's privatization scheme, didn't go nearly far enough. "By banning private hospitals, Mr. Klein is not only stifling innovation and choice, he is making comprehensive reform of the health-care system next to impossible. Alberta's ingenious entrepreneurs—the people who vastly improved the choice, service and price available to Albertans who buy liquor—have been forbidden to put their energy, ideas and money into doing the same for Albertans who are sick."

The *Post's* comparison of health care reform to the province's earlier privatization of liquor sales exposes the shallowness of its analysis, which seems to stem from a knee-jerk adherence to the philosophy that "the free market solves all ills." Booze and health aren't equivalent. Liquor is a simple, easily quantifiable commodity. Health care is a complex and often hazardous basket of goods and services.

Health care requires integration. The Alberta solution just demonstrates that they don't want to understand the problem. I wish I could call it "thoughtless tinkering," but I worry that it is a deliberate attempt to destabilize or destroy medicare.

Many critics of our public system like to argue that Canada is one of the few developed countries resisting the move to a system where more health care is delivered by private operators. Look at Australia, they urge us. Well, I've looked at the various experiments in two-tier health care and I don't like what I see. In Australia, the parallel private system means patients can pay a premium to jump the queue while the public system is left to look after those who can't afford private care.

And notice that these apostles of privatization seldom hold up the United States as an example. As University of British Columbia health economist Robert Evans has put it, "The U.S. is the 'odd man out' of the OECD world, with a unique and uniquely unsatisfactory health care system. Insurance coverage is non-existent for many (between 35 and 40 million), grossly inadequate for many more, and at risk for more yet. Access to and use of these services is as a result highly inequitable, and the health consequences are increasingly documented. Yet costs in the United States, unlike those in any other OECD country, really are 'exploding'; higher than anywhere else and more rapidly." For-profit medicine is less fair and more expensive medicine.

In a comprehensive response to Alberta's Bill 11, Michael Rachlis cited recent articles in the New England Journal of Medicine. Woodlander and Himmelstein found that "for profit" hospitals were 25 per cent per case more expensive than public hospitals—mainly because of escalating administrative costs. In August 1999, the same prestigious medical journal published a paper from Dartmouth University that demonstrated that the more "for profit" hospitals in a community, the higher the health costs to that community.

Rachlis referred to the even more cautionary Woodlander and Himmelstein paper in the July 1999 *Journal of the American Medical Association*, which found that "for profit" health management organizations rated lower than the "not for profit" HMOs on all of the fourteen quality indicators as measured by the National Committee for Quality Assurance. These writers cited a November 1999 study by researchers at Johns Hopkins University that found patients using for-profit dialysis clinics were 20 per cent more likely to die than those attending not-for-profit clinics, and that patients at for-profit clinics were 26 per cent less likely to be referred for kidney transplantation. For-profit medicine is also bad for your health!

The standard argument, of course, is that private clinics will "take the pressure" off the public system. Instead, as the Australian case indicates, they tend to focus on inexpensive procedures such as cataract surgery and ear tube surgery while letting the public system deal with the more difficult and time-consuming cases. My experience of private clinics in Canada is that all the complications and all the after-hours care revert to the public system. The clinics do the easy stuff only during business hours. Even the executive medical clinics seem to focus on costly tests that they can charge for, while tending to neglect the proper history-taking essential to proper primary care. There also seems to be a worrying trend among Canadian specialists towards reserving "slots" for referrals from the private clinics, and even perhaps bumping regular patients to make room for them. One wonders, given present concerns about too few doctors, how moving the best and the brightest to a private second tier could help.

Let me sum up my opposition to privatization clearly: Private health care costs more and is less fair. It is less fair because richer users migrate to the parallel private system, as do many of the best doctors, leaving the rest of us with an inferior public system. The more private health care delivery there is in the system, the greater the total cost. Any doubts about this proposition must be dispelled by taking a cold, hard look at the chaotic, highly inequitable health care situation in the United States, by far the most expensive in the world on a per capita basis.

Private health care breeds bad medicine

If you think the fee-for-service model causes problems in Canada, imagine what it does in the American system, where there are no caps on physician income. It nurtures the kinds of self-referral loops that already harm our health care system, where specialists refer patients from one to another. It tends to increase the number of drugs and the amount of surgery performed, since surgery is a profit centre.

I recently heard a terrible story of an American patient who was given an angiogram the day he was admitted for an amputation because his insurance would cover it. Such procedures are not without risk. Another appalling situation was cited by a Canadian physician when asked why he was leaving the United States to come back to Canada; he stated that he couldn't stand having to see patients in the Emergency Department based on the level of insurance that they had instead of how sick they were.

User fees are useless

Many argue that the only way to save medicare is to introduce user fees for almost every service. User fees look attractive at first glance because they appear to increase revenue while discouraging people from using unnecessary services. In fact, administering user fees usually eats up most or all of the revenue they generate. More important, as Robert Evans has shown, user fees deter the most vulnerable in our society—the poor and the elderly, for example—but don't deter patients who are actually using the system unwisely. We should be concerned that user fees may cause the elderly, the frail, the diabetic, or the pregnant teenager to delay seeking medical attention until they end up in an intensive care unit or with a high-risk pregnancy, problems that will cost the system far more than if they had received timely medical help.

In Saskatchewan, between 1968 and 1971, there was a $1.50 user fee on doctor's visits. Overall, the fee reduced the use of physician services by 6–7 per cent. Among the lowest income levels, physician use went down by 18 per cent. Even the recent $100 annual deductible for seniors' drug prescriptions in Ontario has created problems. Although $100 a year may not sound like a lot of money, a senior with chronic respiratory problems may suffer from recurring acute infections that require a set of costly prescriptions. If the elderly patient doesn't have the hundred dollars, he or she may not fill the prescription. The result may be a critically ill patient in a thousand-dollar-a-day intensive care unit.

I'm afraid I have no use for user fees. They're just a way of avoiding the real problems facing the system, to say nothing about the huge bureaucracy needed to collect them.

What about medical savings accounts?

Some people are very enthusiastic about a proposal to put everyone in Canada on a medical savings plan. This scheme has been tried with some degree of success in health management organizations in the United States, a very different context from the system we have in Canada. It's a financing scheme designed to get patients to use the system less.

As I understand it, this model would operate along the lines of a retirement savings plan, except that your annual contributions would be made by governments, not you. Each year from your birth until you turn sixty-five the government would contribute enough money to your personal plan to cover the average annual cost of health care in Canada. During any given year, many people wouldn't spend a penny of this stipend. Many others would spend only part of it. Any balance in your plan at the end of each year would remain in your account, earning interest and growing in size, a nest egg for your future health care needs. The healthier you were, the bigger your medical savings plan balance would get. If, on the other hand, your health care needs exceeded the amount in your account, a government-funded scheme of catastrophic insurance would kick in to pay for the difference.

The proponents of this idea argue that most users of the system would soon accumulate such a sizeable surplus that they would never need catastrophic insurance, even for acute medical care. They also argue that putting the money for health care directly into the hands of health care consumers would lead to the best of both worlds: a publicly funded system of universal health care in which the discipline of market forces prevail and the customer rules.

Under the medical savings plan model, your reward for staying healthy would be considerable—thus building in a strong incentive for people to use the system more wisely and less often. When you turned sixty-five, any accumulated surplus in your plan would be yours to spend as you wish, money in your pocket. Tax free.

Does this sound too good to be true? I believe it is. It doesn't take into account the role that chance plays in determining who needs medical care: it's not your fault if a car hits you at a crosswalk and you spend lengthy and expensive time in the hospital. Nor does the "average" approach take into account regional variations in who gets sick with what, and how much different treatments cost.

And, what happens if some future government concludes that the savings plans have become too expensive and decides to lower the annual fee? After carefully accumulating your credits by behaving responsibly for years, you might suddenly and arbitrarily be forced to cash them in to get the level of care you once regarded as your basic entitlement. Voilà! Two-tier medicine arrives through the back door and poorer Canadians are left out in the cold.

Medical savings plans may sound good, but I just don't think they would work. They propose an alternative way of financing health care, but have nothing to say about how to deliver it better.

Can we afford to save public health care?

I would answer this question by saying that we can't afford not to. Dr. Sholom Glouberman's paper for the Canadian Policy Research Network on Population Health articulated that the mere existence of a universal health care system is in itself a positive determinant of health. It's not surprising when you think about it: worrying that you might not be able to afford the health care you or a member of your family might need constitutes a major stress that is indeed measurable and deleterious to one's health.

Under the reform model I've proposed in this book—a fully integrated system where the primary-care physician is the coach and the fully informed patient is the captain, and where there is complete horizontal and vertical account-ability—the recent problems of emergency room closures and cancer therapy waiting lists that made headlines in the winter of 1999 and spring of 2000 will evaporate.

Privatization would kill Canadian health care. Compre-hensive, patient-centred reform will cure it. Given the powerful voices and considerable forces arrayed against our public system, achieving reform won't be easy. But I believe Canadians want us to succeed at comprehensive health care reform. They believe deeply in their system of universal health care. Only through their advocacy will politicians find the will to make health care reform happen.

11

Making It Happen

We must act now

The last thing Canadian health care needs is another study of what's wrong and how to fix it. Over the past decade we've studied our system to death. Yet in the spring of 2000, the Senate's committee on social affairs, science, and technology launched a study of the "state of the health care system in Canada." Its report is due in 2002. Enough! We'll kill our system if we don't begin to initiate the sorts of broad reforms I've described in this final part of *Kill or Cure?*. We must act now before it's too late.

There are both positive and negative signs for those who advocate reform. More and more members of the Canadian public are stepping forward to defend our public system and call for reforming it rather than turning it over to the privatizers. The opponents of Alberta's Bill 11 were vocal and effective. They didn't kill the bill but they made their point. From coast to coast, a consensus seems to be emerging among both politicians and ordinary people about the kind of health care system Canadians want.

Those of us on the front lines of the reform movement need to make sure that our message is clear and straightforward. The agenda for reform that I have outlined in this book reduces to the following essential goals:

The Plan

1. **Preserving our values.** To safeguard and enhance the five principles of the Canada Health Act: universality of coverage; equality of access; national portability; comprehensiveness; public funding.

2. **Putting patients first.** To make sure that all reforms serve first and foremost the patient, that access and quality are paramount, and that all Canadians are assured they will get what they need, when they need it.

3. **Establishing shared goals.** To involve Canadians in setting health goals and health service standards and then develop a process through which they can approve performance indicators and review outcomes. The provinces, territories and the professional and voluntary stakeholders must be involved as well.

4. **Focussing on primary care.** To ensure that primary care is delivered in a coordinated fashion as the cornerstone of a fully integrated health care system. In order to accomplish this goal we must secure enough family physician post-graduate positions to be able to return as soon as possible to the optimal 50/50 family doctor/specialist ratio.

5. **Investing in a health infostructure.** To build a health infostructure that will connect all aspects of our health care system, primary care, consultants, pharmacies, labs and hospitals, as well as to provide Canadians with all the information they need to make sound choices about their health and their health care.

6. **Creating true accountability.** To create true accountability founded on complete transparency and constant measuring of outcomes at every level.

7. **Encouraging quality improvement.** To develop a system that encourages continuous quality improvement, including patient satisfaction, and that rewards innovation, responds to diversity, encourages best practices in disease prevention

and health promotion, and includes a strong commitment to the social determinants of health.

The emerging consensus

The Ontario College of Family Physicians has recently put its weight behind a proposed group-practice model that's very close to the one I've described in this book. The Canadian Nurses Association "believes the health system needs to be repaired." They have written to all ministers of health calling for: reform of the health system using primary health care principles as defined by the World Health Organization; expansion of the continuum of care to include home, community, and long-term care; and appropriate use of all health professionals. Among health care professionals and policy-makers, a consensus for reform does seem to be building.

On the ground, where health care providers and policy-makers are grappling directly with the future shape of the system, I discern growing agreement around certain key components of health care reform:

A. Definite agreement
1. Increased investment in out-of-hospital care.
2. Pharmacare—for those not currently covered by public or private plans.
3. Health infostructure.

B. General agreement with notable exceptions
1. Primary care reform.
2. Need for accountability.
3. Reaffirmation of the Canada Health Act.
4. Need for more appropriate incentives to improve quality of care.

C. Still under debate

1. Need for a set of national health goals.
2. Need for national health service standards.
3. Need for a greater focus on prevention and health promotion than on acute care.

There is at least general agreement on most of my health care goals. We have some work to do on Group C, but it's a good start. And I'm encouraged by the broadening base of the reform movement that now includes many of my colleagues in the medical profession, an increasing number of policy analysts, and many advocacy groups. We are all travelling in the same direction. Let's also remind ourselves that our publicly funded system wasn't built in a day. It took decades and many stops and starts before we achieved anything resembling a universal system. A system that really works for the twenty-first century is a few years off. The important thing is to get the process under way now.

This process is far too important to be left to the "experts" inside the health care system or to politicians and bureaucrats at the federal and provincial levels. I believe we must develop a new process, one that will involve all the so-called stakeholders—everyone who is affected by health care reform. Only such broad-based participation will guarantee the national consensus that will make fundamental reform possible.

A new partnership

Before the February 1999 federal Budget, all ten provinces and the territories signed a Health Accord by which they agreed to spend health dollars on health! What a novel idea. Unfortunately, the deal applied only to the 1999 budget. About the same time, a far more important agreement was signed by Ottawa and all the provinces except Quebec, a document entitled "A Framework to Improve the Social Union for Canadians" (SUFA, for short). That agreement provides the basis for a new relationship between the two levels of government. It contains all the mechanisms we need to forge a true federal–provincial partnership in health care and in other supports and services.

SUFA is based on "a mutual respect between orders of government and a willingness to work more closely together to meet the needs of Canadians." Its principles articulate the fundamental values of Canadians—"equality, respect for diversity, fairness, individual dignity and responsibility, and mutual aid and our responsibilities for one another." The signatories promised to "ensure access for all Canadians, wherever they live or move in Canada, to essential social programs and services of reasonable comparable quality." This promise alone implies measuring quality and building accountability. How can we deliver programs of comparable quality from coast to coast without an ability to monitor how well they are being delivered?

SUFA commits the federal government and the provinces and territories to keep Canadians informed. It includes an agreement to monitor and measure outcomes of social programs and report regularly to constituents on the performance of these programs. It includes a commitment to share information and best practices, to support the development of outcome measures, and to work with other governments to develop over time comparable indicators to measure progress on agreed objectives. It promises to involve all Canadians in developing social priorities and reviewing outcomes.

Shortly after SUFA was signed, I chaired a session for the Canadian Society of International Health on World TB Day. There, a WHO official informed me that Canada hadn't submitted its tuberculosis statistics for the previous year because the provinces hadn't yet submitted them to Statistics Canada. This may seem a minor example, but it is symptomatic of a major problem. I believe it is incumbent on both levels of government to honour the commitments they made in SUFA: to produce regular report cards to all Canadians on social outcomes, including health care; and to work towards making the system transparent and accountable. At the present time the federal/provincial/territorial working groups are still behind closed doors, working without proper input from Canadians. I believe that these discussions should be more transparent, so that Canadians can understand what's going on and what's at stake. Let's demonstrate that we can make it work.

But before reform can proceed, we must above all get past the notion that simply throwing more money at health care is the solution. Yes, the provinces may need start-up capital to invest in long-term solutions that are part of comprehensive reform, particularly in the area of new technology. But any such funding must be clearly presented as a long-term commitment to transparency, accountability, and best practices. Let's not fall back into the cycle that characterized the late seventies and early eighties, when governments rashly escalated health spending with no measurable added value.

The provinces and territories must be able to assume their crucial role in reforming medicare. Under our constitution, it is they who carry primary responsibility for health care delivery. The federal government must be the guardian of the basic principles of the system: universality, accessibility, portability. Together with the provinces, territories, stake-holders, and Canadians, it can facilitate the setting of national goals and priorities and take the lead in coordinat-ing national systems for monitoring quality, ensuring accountability, and establishing infostructure—but only in close cooperation with the provinces.

But governments won't act unless Canadians continue to send them the strong message that they believe in our system, that they want it fixed, not replaced.

Carrots and sticks

Studies have shown that a majority of Canadian physicians would embrace an alternative payment system and that the majority of doctors leaving Canada are going to salaried positions elsewhere. Yet some of the leaders of organized medicine continue to blithely ignore these realities. In a speech to the Empire Club in November 1998, Dr. William Orovan, then president of the Ontario Medical Association, made this extraordinary statement: "Ninety per cent of the funding for acute care in Canada is public. This level puts us in the extreme compared to other coun-tries. I believe Canadians would feel very comfortable living with the values of many of these other OECD coun-tries." One wonders where the good doctor gets his infor-mation about the comfort levels of Canadians! I'd say Canadians were proud that we stood first in the public percentage of acute care dollars among OECD countries. Let's keep it that way!

To bring reluctant medical leaders and recalcitrant physi-cians on side, I recommend that we use carrots, not sticks.

The Plan

I like the approach suggested by then Liberal Health critic Gerard Kennedy before the previous Ontario provincial election. He proposed that any group of eight or more doctors who would be prepared to band together to provide 24/7 care should automatically earn the start-up information technology they need and the funding to hire a nurse practitioner for their group practice.

Another attractive incentive might be to enhance pay in return for extra accountability. In a group practice, incentives, even in the form of temporary help, could be provided to help the electronic conversion process.

What can you do?

In the face of what often seem like overwhelming problems, many people throw up their hands helplessly. Yet when it comes to reforming our health care system, I believe that Canadians hold the ultimate power, if only they choose to use it. As I've said many times before, only our belief in our system will save it. I believe with equal conviction that only our voices raised in support of reform will make it happen.

Here's what you can do:

As a patient
- Develop a real relationship with a family doctor.
- Ask good questions about your health care, about prevention, screening, tests, prescriptions, surgery.
- If you have a chronic condition, join a group that provides support and does advocacy for your condition.
- Before you call the doctor or go to an appointment, go through the checklist on page 90.

As an advocate

- If your town is short of doctors, talk to the mayor, write to the provincial minister of health; in the meantime, suggest hiring nurse practitioners.
- Talk to your doctor about primary-care reform; telephone advice; his or her relationship with the local hospital, and with specialists, labs, and pharmacists.
- Write letters to newspapers and politicians.
- Ask why your employer or union doesn't pay a fee for the forms they insist your doctor fill out.
- Find out what's happening at your local hospital. Get involved. Run for a position on the board.
- Be prepared to take on those talking about the need for user fees, privatization, and other simple so-called solutions whether it's in the locker room, at the playground, or on the golf course.
- Find like-minded people, in your neighbourhood, at work, where you volunteer. Form your own advocacy group.

As a citizen

- Insist on input between elections.
- Call your MP and MPP.
- Ask for a town hall meeting on health reform and accountability.
- Push for public involvement under SUFA in the process of "setting social priorities and reviewing outcomes." Remind your MP and your MPP that your governments have committed to this.
- Fight for national standards of care and appropriate health goals.

The Plan

Sister Nuala Kerry, former deputy minister of health in Nova Scotia and professor of ethics at Dalhousie University, has said that although health care may not be a right, it is definitely the duty and obligation of a caring society. I believe that if every Canadian sat down today and wrote his or her personal *Vision Statement for Health Care*, these statements would be remarkably similar. My statement would include:

- The ability to function to my full physical and mental capacity.
- A long-term commitment to health promotion and disease prevention and health research.
- Guaranteed access to high-quality care in a timely fashion.
- A real say in setting, evaluating, and monitoring National Health Service Standards.

This vision statement would emphasize that patients expect to be treated with respect and that health care providers at all levels must be able to do their jobs with pride, knowing that they are participating in a world-class system that is being constantly improved as it responds to the evolving needs of Canadians. It would say that providers must be appreciated and properly remunerated.

Given the information, Canadians can decide what their system would include and how much it needs from the public purse: 9.3 per cent of GDP, as we spend now, or 10 per cent or slightly more. They can decide based on good science and honest handling of the scientific and social evidence. Their values, their faith in democracy, their sense of fairness will prevail over ideologies and moral certainties unsupported by any evidence. Given the choice, Canadians will choose a public system that honours good outcomes, innovation, and creativity, not just the bottom line.

Our health care system is too good to lose. The prospect of real reform is too good to let slip away. Canadians want to make it work. We can get there. We have to, for ourselves and for future generations.

Appendix A

How to Pick a Family Doctor

Check out the doctor's credentials

Doctors come with different credentials. Here's what they mean:

- CCFP (Certified in the College of Family Physicians of Canada). Means either a two-year residency in family medicine and successful completion of certification exams or at least five years in family medicine and successful completion of the certification exams. In order to remain in good standing with the college, fifty hours of continuing medical education must be completed annually.
- FCFP (Fellow in the College of Family Physicians of Canada). Awarded only after a minimum of ten years of practice to holders of the CCFP. A mark of recognition by the doctor's peers.
- Privileges in hospital. Having "active staff" or "courtesy staff" privileges to admit and treat patients in a hospital means that the physician has met the professional standards of the hospital and his or her expertise is recognized as an asset to the institution. Most rural doctors do have hospital privileges; in urban areas it's not as common, but it should be.

- University appointment. Being asked to teach in a medical school is an important indicator of peer review. From large cities to small hamlets there are doctors who hold "lecturer" status at Canadian medical schools. Usually appointments from assistant professor, associate professor, to full professor mean that, at some time, a patient will have the privilege of "teaching" a medical student or a resident. Patient feedback to the supervising physician is an important way to contribute to the future quality of our health care system. However, patients should know that they can always express their discomfort and decline to be seen by a student.

Rate the practice's credentials

Find out as much as you can about the practice before you sign on as a patient.

- How does the practice handle after-hours care? What happens when you call after hours? Can you reach your doctor in a really urgent situation?
- Who will you see when your doctor is away? Ideally this will be a partner in the practice. If not, where will you have to go to be seen? Will your chart be available?
- What hospital is the doctor/practice associated with? Ideally this is a hospital near where you live or one that you can get to easily.
- What staff besides doctors work at the practice? Is there a nurse practitioner or other health care professional on staff?
- What is the waiting room like? You can learn a lot from doctors' waiting rooms. Is it friendly? Do they let you know if you're going to have a long wait?
- Does the practice have a newsletter or a patient manual?
- Are certain services charged for? Is there an annual fee?

Interview the doctor

- Can we talk? Your first appointment with a new family doctor is your chance to interview him or her. Bells should go off if you leave the office without asking the questions you wanted to ask. Equally important, did the doctor ask the questions you wanted to hear? The most crucial of these is the open-ended one posed just before you leave: "Is there anything else you wanted to ask/know, etc." The open-ended question is the one that will trigger the question you hesitated to ask, or forgot to ask.

- Do I feel judged? Would I trust this person with personal secrets? If you'd be afraid to tell this person that you're having an affair, or that you're gay, then this is not the doctor for you.

- Would you feel comfortable sending the rest of your family to see this doctor? Each member of your family must feel confident that personal confidences are treated confidentially, whether it's a teenager asking about the pill or marital problems. (A great family doctor will often persuade a family member that he or she would indeed feel better if personal confidences were being shared with the family.)

- Will this doctor discuss your concerns about other family members with you? A real "family" doctor will listen to your questions about other family members—without, of course, ever revealing confidential information. Such a doctor can often eliminate your worries about an out-of-town family member by a reassuring comment.

- What about alternative practitioners? Does this doctor slam the door the minute you mention chiropractors, massage therapists, acupuncturists, or naturopaths? Or is he or she open to alternative practitioners and therapies? Does this doctor ever refer patients to non-medical health care providers?

Appendix A

Rate the practice over time. Train your doctor

No practice is perfect, and once you've signed on and become familiar with your doctor and the others in the office, any flaws will become more apparent. The only way doctors and the practice get better is if patients are willing to train them.

- Do you feel looked after? Not only by your doctor, but by the whole team? Are your phone calls returned? Are you treated politely? Do you secure prompt appointments for true emergencies? Are you getting the information you need? (This is where things like a practice newsletter, basic information on x-ray preparation, cancelling appointments, and so on, come in handy.)
- Do you feel that you've been taken care of? As an individual with your own personal characteristics, worries? As a family member? As a member of a community?
- Are you reminded when it's time for a check-up, etc.?
- Do you feel like you're in charge? Do you have the final say—whether it's declining chemotherapy or choosing a home birth with a midwife? The doctor–patient relationship must allow the partners to agree to respectfully disagree. The relationship is not about control.

I always thought that it was fair game for the patient to ask me what I would do in their circumstance. I would always explain that my situation would be different, but would be honest in my response, given those differences.

How to Become a Health Care Advocate

The following contact information is organized under four headings: Action, Advocacy, Analysis, Using the System. It will provide you with a wealth of resources for information and advocacy.

Action

Prime Minister of Canada

www.pm.gc.ca

The current prime minister is Jean Chrétien. His National Forum on Health, which reported in 1997, identified the key challenges facing our health care system. The National Forum on Health can be contacted at www.nfh.hc-sc.gc.ca

Minister of Health

www.hc-sc.gc.ca/english/minister.htm

The current federal health minister is Allan Rock. His main priority is to preserve and strengthen Canada's medicare system through partnership with his provincial and territorial counterparts.

The Opposition Parties

The opposition parties have different approaches to solving

health care problems. They are often in a position to ask questions in Question Period to put the health minister on the record. Influencing their policy process can also be important.

Canadian Alliance
www.canadianalliance.gc.ca

Bloc Québécois
www.blocquebecois.org/

New Democratic Party
www.ndp.ca

Progressive Conservative Party
www.pcparty.ca

Members of the House of Commons and Senators
www.parl.gc.ca

Provincial and Territorial Governments and Health Ministries
Newfoundland www.gov.nf.ca
Nova Scotia www.gov.ns.ca
New Brunswick www.gov.nb.ca
Prince Edward Island www.gov.pe.ca
Quebec www.gouv.qc.ca
Ontario www.gov.on.ca
Manitoba www.gov.mb.ca
Saskatchewan www.gov.sk.ca
Alberta www.gov.ab.ca
British Columbia www.gov.bc.ca
Nunavut www.gov.nu.ca
Northwest Territories www.gov.nt.ca
Yukon www.gov.yk.ca

Advocacy

Friends of Medicare
www.friendsofmedicare.ab.ca
The Friends of Medicare is a voluntary, non-profit Alberta-based coalition of individuals, service organizations, social justice groups, unions, associations, churches, and community organizations. It was incorporated in September 1979 in response to mounting threats to medicare.

Canadian Health Coalition
www.healthcoalition.ca
The Canadian Health Coalition was founded in 1979 to address service cutbacks and funding changes in the health care system. Its membership includes senior citizens, trade unions, church groups, women's organizations, and health care providers.

Consumers' Association of Canada
www.consumer.ca
Consumers' Association of Canada is an independent, non-profit volunteer organization which represents and informs consumers, and advocates action on their behalf to improve the quality of life. Wendy Armstrong, past president of the Alberta office, has been particularly engaged in the fight against Bill 11. For more information, go to www.ecn.ab.ca/consumer

Health Action Lobby
www.cna-nurses.ca/heal
Formed in 1991, the Health Action Lobby (HEAL) is a coalition of national health and consumer associations dedicated to protecting and strengthening Canada's health care system. Its founding members include: Canadian Association

for Community Care, Canadian Healthcare Association, Canadian Home Care Association, Canadian Medical Association, Canadian Nurses Association, Canadian Psychological Association, Canadian Public Health Association, and Consumers Association of Canada.

Council of Canadians
www.canadians.org
Founded in 1985, the Council of Canadians describes itself as a non-partisan citizens' watchdog organization. With fifty chapters across the country, it organizes national campaigns on issues including health care.

Save Medicare!
www.savemedicare.com
This is a grassroots information resource for people and organizations concerned about the growing threat to the national medicare program in Canada. The organization shares the site with Youth for Medicare.

Canadian Association of Physicians for the Environment
www.cape.ca/index.html
CAPE is an organization for health professionals concerned about Ecosystem Health, Human Health and Sustainable Development. It addresses issues of local and global environmental degradation by educating members, policy makers, and the general public and by working with other groups with similar concerns.

Medical Reform Group
www.web.net/~mrg
The Medical Reform Group is a voluntary association of socially concerned physicians and medical students who

emphasize the social, political, and economic forces shaping health and health care in Canada. Membership is open to non-physicians.

Canadian Medical Association
www.cma.ca
Founded in 1867, the Canadian Medical Association is the professional association for physicians. On behalf of its members, it advocates for access to quality health and health care as well as change within the medical profession.

Canadian Nurses Association
www.can-nurses.ca
Dating from 1908, the Canadian Nurses Association is the professional association representing a federation of approximately 110,000 registered nurses. Its goal is to advance the quality of nursing by promoting high standards of practice, education, research, and administration.

College of Family Physicians of Canada
www.cfpc.ca
Founded in June 1954, the College of Family Physicians is a national medical association supporting family physicians. It currently has a voluntary membership of over 13,000 family physicians in ten provincial chapters across the country. It seeks to promote high-quality health care by encouraging and supporting high standards of medical education at all levels.

Appendix B
Analysis

Canadian Policy Research Network
www.cprn.org
CPRN began in 1995 as a non-profit organization. It acquires its funding from diverse sources such as federal and provincial governments, foundations, and corporations. It operates by creating networks of expertise from universities, think-tanks, and other bodies.

Caledon Institute
www.caledoninst.org
Established in 1992, the Caledon Institute of Social Policy is a private, non-profit think-tank supported primarily by the Toronto-based Maytree Foundation. The Caledon Institute of Social Policy does research and analysis seeking to inform and influence public opinion and to foster public discussion on social policy.

Canadian Centre for Policy Alternatives
www.policyalternatives.ca
This economic and social policy think-tank was established in 1980 by academic and labour economists to provide a counterbalance to the Fraser and C.D. Howe institutes. It engages in many health-related activities.

Parkland Institute
www.ualberta.ca/~parkland
The Parkland Institute, situated at the University of Alberta, is a broad-based, provincial research organization, supported by academics, private businesses, unions, and professional, community, and religious organizations. It conducts and publishes research on economic, social, cultural, and political issues as well as sponsoring conferences and colloquia.

Fraser Institute
www.fraserinstitute.ca
Founded in 1974, the Fraser Institute is an economic think-tank that aims to redirect public attention to the role markets can play in providing for the economic and social well-being of Canadians. It is financed by the sale of its publications and the contributions of its members.

Canadian Institute for Health Information
www.cihi.ca
CIHI is a federally chartered but independent, non-profit organization that provides health information and analysis needed to make sound health decisions. The general public can be a client along with ministries of health, health care facilities, health-related organizations and associations, the research community, and the private sector.

Using The System

The Canadian Health Network
www.canadian-health-network.ca
The Canadian Health Network is a national, bilingual Internet-based health information service, funded by and in partnership with Health Canada. CHN connects Canadians to high-quality local, regional, and national health information and resources in partnership with over 500 non-profit health organizations across Canada.

PISCES: Partnering in Self-Help Community Education and Support
www.pisces.on.ca
PISCES assists groups in their contribution to the quality of life of people with cancer. PISCES training programs help cancer patients gain skills in communication, problem-solving,

advocacy and self-help group facilitation. PISCES training programs for doctors and other health care professionals increase communications skills and self-help group facilitation.

Women's Health Matters
www.womenshealthmatters.ca
A source for reliable, evidence-based, and up-to-date information on women's health. The information on this site is brought to you by the women's health experts at Sunnybrook and Women's College Health Sciences Centre and the Centre for Research in Women's Health.

Select Bibliography

Books

Bliss, Michael. *William Osler: A Life in Medicine*. Toronto: University of Toronto Press, 1999.

Dorland, John L., and S. Mathwin Davis, eds. *How Many Roads . . . ? Regionalization and Decentralization in Health Care*. Kingston: Queen's University School of Policy Studies, 1996.

Foot, David. *Boom, Bust & Echo 2000*. Toronto: Macfarlane Walter & Ross, 1996, 1998.

Heeney, Helen. *Life Before Medicare: Canadian Experiences*. Toronto: Ontario Coalition of Senior Citizens Organizations, 1995.

Picard, André. *Critical Care: Canadian Nurses Speak for Change*. Toronto: HarperCollins/A Phyllis Bruce Book, 2000.

Priest, Lisa. *Operating in the Dark: The Accountability Crisis in Canada's Health Care System*. Toronto: Doubleday Canada, 1998.

Reports, Studies, Articles, Documents

Advisory Council on Health Infostructure. *Connecting for Better Health: Strategic Issues (Interim Report)*. Ottawa: Minister of Public Works and Government Services, 1998.

Albert, Terry, and Eden Cloutier. *The Economic Burden of Unintentional Injury in Ontario*. Toronto: SMARTRISK, 1999.

Select Bibliography

Auditor General of Canada. "Federal Support of Health Care Delivery." Chapter 29 in *Report of the Auditor General to the House of Commons of Canada*. November 1999. Ottawa: Public Works and Government Services Canada, 1999.

Bégin, Monique. "How I'd fix health care." *Policy Options Politique*. May 2000, p. 7.

Brown, Adalsteinn D., et al. *Accountability in Health Care: Results of an OECD Ministry of Health and Related Organizations Survey*. Toronto: University of Toronto Department of Health Administration, 2000.

Canadian Institute for Health Information. *Health Care in Canada: First Annual Report*. Ottawa: Canadian Institute for Health Information, 2000.

Canadian Medical Association. *The Future of Health and Health Care in Canada: Restoring Access to Quality Health Care*. Ottawa: Canadian Medical Association, 1996.

Douglas, Angus E., et al. *Sustainable Health Care for Canada (Synthesis Report)*. Kingston and Ottawa: Queen's-University of Ottawa Economic Projects, 1995.

Federal, Provincial and Territorial Advisory Committee on Population Health. *Toward a Healthy Future: 2nd Report on the Health of Canadians*. Ottawa: Public Works and Government Services Canada, 1999.

Flood, Colleen M. "Accountability, flexibility, and integration." *Policy Options Politique*. May 2000, p. 17.

Government of Canada. *A Framework to Improve the Social Union for Canadians* [online]. [Cited June].
www.hc-sc.gc.ca/english/archives/releases/age6bk.htm

Leatt, Peggy, ed. HealthcarePapers: *Organizing Primary Care for an Integrated System*. Toronto: Ontario Hospital Quarterly, 1999.

Macdonald, J. K., et al. *An Inventory and Analysis of Accountability Practices in the Canadian Health System*. Report submitted to Health Canada by Queen's Health Policy, September 1999.

National Forum on Health. *Canada Health Action: Building on the Legacy (Final Report of the National Forum on Health)*. Ottawa: Minister of Public Works and Government Services, 1997.

Naylor, David. "Health Care in Canada: Incrementalism Under Fiscal Duress; Fiscal constraints have eroded Canadians' enthusiasm about their single-payer system, but their commitment to universal coverage is holding firm." *Health Affairs*, May–June 1999.

Organization for Economic Cooperation and Development. *OECD Health Data 99: A Comparative Analysis of 29 Countries.* Paris: OECD, 1999.

Rachlis, Michael, and Carol Kushner. *Primary Health Care in Canada: A Report for the Health Transition Fund, Health Canada.* Toronto: Unpublished, 1997.

Schafer, Arthur. "Ignorance and Uncertainty in Medicine." *Globe and Mail*, January 9, 1990, p. A7.

Statistics Canada. *Health Reports*. Ottawa: Statistics Canada, Catalogue 82-003, various dates.

Statistics Canada. "How Healthy Are Canadians?" Special issue of *Health Reports*, vol. 11, no. 3, March 31. Ottawa: Public Works and Government Services Canada, 2000.

Tyrrell, Lorne, and Dale Dauphinée. *Task Force on Physician Supply in Canada*. Ottawa: Canadian Medical Forum Task Force, 1999.

United Nations Development Program. *Human Development Report 1999*. New York: Oxford University Press, 1999.

World Health Organization. *World Health Report 2000*. Copyright World Health Organization, 2000. Available at *www.who.int*

Acknowledgements

I used to describe my Toronto family practice as a small-town practice in the middle of a big city. From the poorest to the richest, my patients taught me much of what I know about how to be a family doctor. Thankfully many of these former patients live in my Toronto riding of St. Paul's and have maintained our partnership in my new role as a member of Parliament. And there are my new constituents, too many to mention, who every day demonstrate what it means to take seriously their civic responsibilities. They are people who care deeply about how political decisions are made and want a say in those decisions.

I'd like to thank Sally Tindal, who first suggested I should write down what I've been saying for years, and Jeffrey Simpson for making me mad enough to do it! I'm grateful to Valerie Hussey, who pointed me to my agent, Dean Cooke, who helped develop the concept for the book and find the publisher.

Phyllis Bruce, my editor at HarperCollins, provided calm, compassionate, insightful, and professional advice at every stage of the writing and editing process. She gave me the confidence to see the project through to completion. The talented, understanding, and extremely patient Rick Archbold still can't read my writing but he can certainly read my

Acknowledgements

mind. I've appreciated both his professionalism and his sense of humour.

I must also pay tribute to the heroes who inspire me almost daily—Monique Bégin, Doris Anderson, Ursula Franklin, and Jane Jacobs. Special thanks to a very special group of friends that Rick refers to as my Brain Trust— Mary Eberts, Brian Gamble, Gerard Kennedy, and Pat McNamara. Their mark is on almost every page of this book. (Of these, Mary Eberts deserves an extra-special thank you for her painstaking work on the final manuscript to make sure that her tough questions posed over years of Sunday morning breakfasts were properly answered.) Tony Marcil and his son Jeff helped me hone and support my arguments. Ellen Hodnett, Heather MacLean, David Naylor, and Walter Rosser, both teachers and colleagues, have greatly influenced my thinking. Barbara Hall, Bill Inwood, Colin Mackenzie, and others too numerous to mention have been hugely supportive. Michael Decter, Colleen Flood, Cal Gutkin, Carol Kushner, Michael Rachlis, and Arthur Schafer have willingly shared their observations and values.

At the Research Branch of the Library of Parliament, I have had the invaluable support and insight of Bill Young and the priceless generosity and health expertise of Nancy Miller-Chénier. Parliamentary colleagues such as Bill Graham, John Godfrey, Sheila Finestone, and Paul Martin, who all love ideas and finding solutions, fuel my optimism. Also in Ottawa, Chaviva Hozek, Jonathan Murphy, Paul Genest, and Greg Loyst have been always there to answer that one last question. My former colleagues at Bedford Medical Associates, especially Tina Currie, Rae Lake, Jean Marmoreo, and Darlene Roth, provided a fantastic laboratory in which to develop a patient-centred model of care. I've also gained important insights from several who work in the private sector, especially Mary Jo Dunlop, Dr. David Imrie, and Dr. Ramesh Zacharias. I owe a very special thank you to Ian Delaney and Margarita Trujillo at Sherritt International Corporation, who provided huge support as I scrambled with the proofs while attending the International Association of Health Policy meeting in Havana. Et je remercie Germaine Paré, mon professeur de français. Grâce à elle, mes journées à Ottawa commencent généralement sous le signe de la confiance en soi et de la bonne humeur.

One of the privileges of being a member of Parliament is having such a capable and enthusiastic staff: Tricia Geddes, Esther Shron, Sarah Fink, Leanne Maidment, and Josh Arnold. They let me take the credit for much of what they do.

The founders of Women's College Hospital continue to inspire me with their vision. The present-day leaders of Friends of Women's College continue to inspire me with their commitment to patient-centred care: Marilou McPhedran, Joc Palm, Gail Regan, and Bev Richardson.

This list of acknowledgements would be incomplete without a mention of the place where much of this book was thought through and worked on: the majestic and humbling Georgian Bay, where I find serenity and a sense of perspective.

My parents, Jack and Eunice Bennett; my husband, Peter O'Brian; and my sons, Jack and Ben, continue to amaze me with their support, even though I too often take them for granted. And lastly, a word of tribute to my late Aunt Mil. She taught me very early that if you just ask other people questions and listen to the answers, wonderful things can happen!

C B

Index

Index

Index